Simping

A Practical Guide to Healthy Relationships

(How to Stop Simping and Make Any Woman Fall Down on Her Knees)

Edward Webster

Published By **Tyson Maxwell**

Edward Webster

Simping: A Practical Guide to Healthy Relationships (How to Stop Simping and Make Any Woman Fall Down on Her Knees)

ISBN 978-1-9994868-7-7

Legal & Disclaimer

The information contained in this book is not designed to replace or take the place of any form of medicine or professional medical advice. The information in this book has been provided for educational & entertainment purposes only.

The information contained in this book has been compiled from sources deemed reliable, and it is accurate to the best of the Author's knowledge; however, the Author cannot guarantee its accuracy and validity and cannot be held liable for any errors or omissions. Changes are periodically made to this book. You must consult your doctor or get professional medical advice before using any of the suggested remedies, techniques, or information in this book.

Upon using the information contained in this book, you agree to hold harmless the Author from and against any damages, costs, and expenses, including any legal fees potentially resulting from the application of any of the information provided by this guide. This disclaimer applies to any damages or injury caused by the use and application, whether directly or indirectly, of any advice or information presented, whether for breach of contract, tort, negligence, personal injury, criminal intent, or under any other cause of action.

You agree to accept all risks of using the information presented inside this book. You need to consult a professional medical practitioner in order to ensure you are both able and healthy enough to participate in this program.

Table Of Contents

Chapter 1: Three Answers

Everybody in the society is trying to steer at you which mean that your desires as a man of 18 are not important to their goals. When it comes to the questions you've had in the forefront of your thoughts then, we'll look at matters from all perspectives, before analyzing the subject objectively before arriving to the root of the issue.

It is evident that the left-leaning "red pills" and"blue pills" that are left leaning "blue pills" have a polar opposite regarding the majority of issues. However, even in cases which they can agree with regards to scientific or psychological facts but they offer opposite strategies. So, in the text, we encourage you to think inward and not look outward to find solutions you want.

Red Pills and Blue Pills

The red pill is divided is an overstatement. The red pill has passionate supporters on one side as well as those who compare it with capital or violent crime on the other. There are people who rely on it, as well as women who hate it completely. Some consume the pill daily throughout the day. There are those who stop taking it, and "detox" of it's "misogynist harmful negative effects."

Blue pill pushed by powerful institutions that include mainstream media as well as Hollywood and, in essence, all guardians of virtue and culture have a stake in it. It's the reason why those with opinions that aren't in the mainstream have to bear an enormous social price in order to stand out from the crowd. Some critics from the blue pill argue that it's contrary to the society which affirms the value of individual freedom as well as freedoms.

The problem with every set of concepts is that at one point they can't exist without a context yet at the same time they are affected by the other thoughts in their surroundings, until they reach the point where they have lost the essence of what they are. The people who are against the red pill idea are often taking advantage of this fact to denounce it, remove its existence from the world and denigrate those who adhere to its sensible ideas as being sexist. Naturally, red pills are given an overall negative reputation.

The red pill's adherent who tells males to appreciate their own worth and get more from their relationships could be considered a radical and crazy person who believes the law should legalize gender-based violence Then the entire discussion is cut off. The red pill often claims of this as an untruthful strategy that is used deliberately by blue pills to denigrate them, and it's quite easy to fall for. When you read the book, we urge that you keep your sanity to avoid falling into traps in which one's side's position is judged against its weakest components.

Blue pills, in their own way think that they have the moral responsibility to dissipate beliefs of the red pill by whatever method necessary. This is because red pills can be extremely dangerous as well as corrupting innocent males. This is why they have been referred to by the red pill as "hypocrites" due to their tendency to hold men and women to a different standard, and still at time proclaiming to be the the arbiters of equality. There is another trap you need to stay clear of - the notion which says "if women can take part in this, why can't males?" That can help in winning arguments on a discussion forum but it's not going to aid in getting what you need from women.

In this publication, we take an impartial look at some of the controversial views regarding men and their relationships today. We examine the way these concepts are debated in different circles of society. Then, we put the main argument under the microscope and decide on what we think is the most acceptable as well as which are ones we feel need to be revisited.

The only criteria we have is that we must consider: if the idea is ethically sound that is internally consistent and practical within the context of our world, and the psychological profile of a man can be attributed to it, then we'll support the idea.

What we are referring to with intellectual honesty is the idea must be common sense that it doesn't take a obscure, obscure, or false-intellectual route to arrive at the predetermined conclusion.

What we are referring to by internal logical consistency is this concept is not built on the basis of a dual standards, in which it is applied the same way in one situation however, it is the reverse when it comes to the following setting. This is essential to avoid having contradictory behavior instructions.

Practicality within the context of our culture is that we don't accept concepts based on how high, "right," or "moral" they may be but rather, we accept their relevance based on the way their application in the real world in the context of the dynamic that each of us experiences every day on a daily basis.

In the context of the psychological makeup of a person means we shouldn't tell ourselves what we're like. We, without an appropriate term are actually primitive creatures. Any platitude "wokeness," education, Denialism, forward-thinking bargaining, compromise or whatever else you can think of will eliminate your basic caveman nature.

No, we're talking about violence, or other illegal or deviant conduct in this discussion. This is about the way individuals are genetically programmed to provide defense the position of dominance and be competitive in their sexuality to ensure that they pass on their genetics. Our advice is different from the traditional tendency to advise men to take away their inherent nature. This is only done only if it's in their favor.

The red pill is included in our view because it's beneficial in certain situations. Many people may believe it's because the pill is a weapon to pit men against women, it's far from the truth. After doing lots of study, we've discovered that the pill actually pits males against each other. The red pill rests on the assumption that there's an actual competition that men play with other males to gain the best women.

On the other hand, women typically have a choice of males from the beginning. Their difficulty isn't finding the right man, but rather in overcoming the temptation to choose the wrong guy. Women have the right to make their own choosing. Males, on the other hand need to locate an attractive woman. And contrary to what popular culture would have you believe that they're hard to locate - which is why there's fierce competition.

Blue pills enjoy the benefit of widespread acceptance, however they have their shortcomings. They typically argue based on the premise that they believe to be ethically adamant. They usually take the form of statements which everyone should accept as truthful, and serve to be the basis of all discussions that follow (see the section about framing).

You may be familiar with blue pill claim that people who don't have "girl parts" isn't entitled to opinions on specific issues. If this is the case, any viewpoint one could or might not share that's not similar to their own is invalid as null and void. It's as if there's nothing to discuss which is your choice to go the way they want. Another trap that to avoid when you read the book. Anything or anything is subject to scrutiny.

What to Expect From This Book

This book is intended for males who wish to open up about their true desires from women, and not be intimidated by social norms that are changing to choose something is something they don't want to live with in order to considered "open-minded."

This book can also be used by women who wish to speak truthfully about themselves regarding the worth they bring to males, and what they expect to men. Instead of trying to force men to change their codes to meet the ideal of progress on paper but is a sabotage to the fundamental human instincts.

The book isn't for those who are looking to win a social debate or appear smarter than those on the other group. This book is not intended for those who are averse to hate or who want to engage in thoughts that cause hatred. This is a program for those looking for a partner who they can live with within a lasting partnership that combines wisdom gained over time as well as shared values and an attraction to each other and respect.

This book follows the format of a question and answer. Every chapter begins with a thesis statement and then examines the argument for and against it, and finally, cuts into the nonsense and exposes the truth out. The chapters are unpretentious in the way the questions are addressed since we believe the honesty of oneself is the key to a positive or satisfying relationship. This is what we're aiming at here, not just to be able to tell you what's right or to tell you what you ought to feel however, we want to be able to admit the way you feel and remind you that your innermost feelings exist because of a reason.

We hope your travels through the pages of this blog will prove informative, insightful, giving positive. In the end, we wish you to discover the things you value most and what you desire from your relationships and that all of your life's important choices will be grounded on the ground, not made based on what somebody or someone else who has an agenda will tell you what that you should value.

Chapter 2: Are There Alpha And Beta Males, And Which One Am I?

Red Pill Take

The entire idea of alpha and beta males was born out of an idea of the "seduction group" (meaning people who are pick-up artists) in the red pill concept this concept is now used to mean the traits which make men attractive or undesirable to potential partners.

Alpha males are viewed as someone who takes the reigns and creates the reality he sees While a beta man is viewed as one who lets the world rule himself and determine his own reality. Alpha males choose to dominate throughout his life. A beta male is controlled by females and males through choice, or because of the habit of complacency. Alpha characteristics may be present natural in certain men due to of their body or nature, however the man has the option of choosing to be an alpha male by putting in at achieving those vital characteristics.

Beta males let everyone else walk over his body, but he continues giving his time, energy as well as physical assets to people (particularly women) hoping that they reciprocate at their own discretion. This generosity, however, negatively influences how potential partners view the person, so it is inevitable that he will be disappointed.

If a person is Alpha or Beta his character is across a broad spectrum. Alphas have a tendency to be "more than alpha" in comparison to others, and certain betas tend to be "more beta" as compared to other. The position of a man within the spectrum can depend on his competition pool. That means weak alphas may be perceived as more positive in the absence of stronger alphas included in the equation. But, in today's interconnected world, women are able to connect to huge pools of potential male companions, which means that males can't go around in claiming to be an alpha. You just have to be working for it to become one.

Blue Pill Take

Males who are beta and alpha males have been the creation of the right-wing, pick-up artist men, and toxic guys to turn beautiful young men into feminists. Women may find aspects like confidence attractive but men with a shy, sensitive personality are just as attractive. In addition, the traits of dominantness, aggression assertiveness, dominance, and exiguous are toxic and must be regulated for males to have a society that is equal.

Instead of trying to be dominating, those who wish to improve their standing among women must be able to distinguish themselves through seeking out fame (i.e.

being accomplished, successful, polished). Submissive men who are polished and accomplished looks better than an overbearing male who is less polished.

No BS Take

The beta vs alpha male concept may be a bit silly at times and may not be a good idea, but it works as a simple framework for knowing the different male characteristics, and the way women see them within a classroom setting however, in actual life. If you are analyzing something is a good idea to use some kind of framework, rather than use one. Anyone who is unhappy with the "alpha and beta" framework can suggest a new framework. and then put it on the market to see if it gets a response.

There is a lot of talk about women expressing a preference for men who are less dominant however, the reality suggests the reverse. Women appear to prefer Alphas in the first place. It is confirmed by scientific research in evolutionary biology.

Females are drawn to confident, self-assured males with attractive physiques which is the alpha male. The women do appreciate alphas but they also be taught to appreciate betas. Women who are actively seeking for men who have beta characteristics tend to do it not because of instinct or as a result of negative experiences they had when dealing with males who have alpha traits. This means that they've been injured previously, so they're selecting a beta for an emotional security or self-esteem boost.

It's not saying that, if you have qualities that could be thought to be beta-like, you shouldn't be prepared for a life of waiting for "sloppy moments." In regards to appeal to females it's like being the stock in an index. It is possible to go either between high and low and have the ability to exert influence over a variety of factors that impact your worth.

The best way to present yourself is to prepare your self for success on the world of dating by portraying yourself as a lively and resourceful partner (i.e. possessing a good job name and looking like you is able to pay the money and so on). These are all signs of respectability. particularly important when you're in search of a long-term partnership However, if you're looking to be a romantic it is best to maximize these "animalistic qualities" that include dominance, aggressiveness as well as physical attractiveness. I guarantee you that in the current single-night-out culture when you're outspoken and a jobless man is more likely to get laid than a smooth-talking, scrawny and well-mannered Sales VP.

Beta male can be described as the word "insult," but when you've got the characteristics that make you one, consider the experience as a way to get off rather than a lifetime sentence. Also, it's important to be proud of your own worth. Do not settle for someone who has unachievable burdens just because you believe you've got none options. Be selective as well. At times, it is important to wait your time and refrain from making any definitive decisions until you've positioned your self correctly.

Nobody wants to consider themselves beta. It wouldn't be a wise idea to use any guidelines to determine "betaness." Yet the best approach is to assess all of your shortcomings and strive to continuously and diligently make each one better. Do not let blue pills fool you into a false sense of security in the belief that you're blessed with "inner attractiveness." Do your effort. There's no way to go to go about this.

Chapter 3: Should I Be Persistent With Women?

Red Pill Take

For the red pill and especially to the pickup artist kind There are two kinds of persistence: the correct kind and the unsuitable type. The correct kind of perseverance can help a man get over the resistance by the woman at the beginning of the relationship. It will help him to get acceptance. A lack of persistence can put the man in a bind and increases the likelihood to end up in the so-called friend zone. For a better understanding of the two begin by identifying the wrong determination.

This type of insistence is evident in situations where instead of inviting for a date immediately and asking for her contact number, or makes a casual connection with her but does not state his proposition in the initial instance. The result is commonly referred to as "follow-up mode" as he needs to contact her to give him an opportunity to present his case.

The man will soon end up on the downwards slope, in which he continues to ask for her attention, but she is always declining or even putting the off. At this point it becomes more difficult to attract her attention and the harder she tries to lose the little interest she may be feeling towards him in the beginning.

Following a period of time spent communicating after which the man might realize that they already have a good rapport between each other for her to begin thinking about him as a friend at which point she might begin to dump the emotional burden upon him or inviting him to join her in sexy physical work (manual work).

Persistence that is right is to ask the girl immediately (no hesitation) and using well-trained "game" techniques to get beyond her doubt or resistance. In other words, instead of asking her for contacts, he ought to just do it and request her to chat immediately on a casual date, but one however. If he can succeed by this method this will give him more control over the event. If he proposes to her for a simple, easy fast, no-pressure date, she'll not be tempted to think about the issue, making her more likely to not be sloppy.

In the end, your first interaction with her is an ideal time to keep going. Do your best to come up with an acceptable solution for any arguments she might throw at you, however make sure that you're not grumpy about it to ensure she doesn't feel like she's being pushed around. If she does end staying with her contacts but not agreeing to a relationship but the persistence can make the experience unforgettable, which will put you over every other person she's had a conversation with.

Blue Pill Take

Blue pill's view on perseverance can be summed by a well-known saying that says "no is the same as no." According to the committed feminists, having a woman tell you no repeatedly is considered sexual discrimination. Many believe that when you've been told "No," you should acknowledge it, apologize in a heartfelt way and then bow respectfully and never bring the subject back up. Some blue pills consider that you have earned an opportunity to invite to meet her again and months or many years later when you've built an rapport or establish a relationship with her following the initial rejection and she's suggested to consider it. In this scenario there is no way to stop from contacting her to inquire about some power relations in play between the two of you.

The notion that you could "wear the woman down" through persistently calling to see her has been propagated by the media for a lengthy time as per blue pills. It's a result that can be very stressful for women. The persistence of women is extremely unprofessional, stressful as well as emotionally draining for women. Therefore, you must stop now.

Additionally, there are situations where women might be able to be able to say "yes" however she says"no. This is due to social expectations. are conditioned women to be courteous and warm, but sometimes women are scared of what could happen if reject a man. Are they likely to lose friends? Do they lose their job? They could be portrayed as a vulgar?

A desire for politeness could make a woman not all that attracted by the idea of a guy to accept to the prospect of a date. If you find that the "yes" that you get doesn't seem to be enthusiastic enough, perhaps it's time to try to be the best you can to secure that huge benefit of a date that she's been begging for you. And if you don't get it you should leave in the most gracious manner that is possible.

No BS Take

Alright. There are many ways to reach out to women. There are a lot of possibilities for women to decline your request regardless of whether your manner was flawless in accordance with whatever criteria for dating or picking up you choose to use. As you move into a relationship, don't consider any "no" as an personal attack that you have to combat all the fibers that you are. Sometimes, the reasons behind declining may not have anything to have anything to do with you in any way or there may be a plethora of things going on within her world that you're completely unaware of.

At the beginning the first step is to recognize the fact that her reaction is likely be based upon her impressions, not based on yours. Therefore, during the course of your interaction it's important to determine the direction she's coming from and also what her thoughts are in the present. Put the best effort in regards to your appearance (how you appear, what you speak about, whether you're exuding confidence by your body language, etc.). It is also advisable to invite her to a conversation after having a chat with her a little or at a point in which she's showing your humor. It is best to ask within the context of a casual conversation. the question shouldn't appear suddenly, and shouldn't be out of the norm.

In response to her question to you, don't simply listen to hear the words "yes" as well as "no." It is important be attentive to the words she's actually using. Females always want to elaborate on their thoughts, which will provide an understanding of the extent to which you're allowed the ability to continue.

If the "no" has clearly stated "barrier to a"yes", ,"--for example, if she states "I am not able to go out with you due to ABC ,"--then it is your responsibility to continue to offer a viable alternative to overcome that obstacle. The solution you propose should be based upon her needs rather than your own.

If she continues to make absurd excuses, it is important be aware of the tone and body language she uses as well as her body of voice. If she is playful then you should continue to keep up with her playfulness. If she seems friendly but firm and gentle, then you must beg off, but you should leave the discussion with a positive attitude. If she displays a creeping upwards level of aggression, then bounce or find someone else you can attack her.

If you do, don't make the mistake of sour grapes Never yell at her. Take a moment to leave with a positive phrase and with your head held at a high level, and let her imagine what she's not getting. Be assured that she's likely to ask questions.

Persistence could be perceived as bullying if a girl isn't in the proper mindset for the discussion. The biggest mistake young guys commit is panicking when they think of the encounter ending in rejection. Their persistent behavior can take on an anger or defensive tone which can be a huge turnoff.

If you're so shocked from that "no" that you're unable to concentrate it is better moving on, rather instead of playing a weak perseverance game, which makes you appear as a whiny small twit.

If you're trapped by the number and not a concrete date, suggest an interesting informal, fun, and adventurous trip with a partner, and in an time which is most likely to work for her.

If she rejects the offer then steer the conversation to her choice of location, time, and date of the event. This type of check date suggestion could work for you since it offers her an opportunity to participate in something she's wanted to try for some time.

If she reverts back towards you and tells you that she is happy after the guy makes the decision or not, she may have accidentally signed up to go out for an evening with you. Contact your brain trust to plan your date.

Chapter 4: Should I Collect Notch (Sexual Conquests)? Red Pill Take

The accumulation of notches could be positive or good thing, based on the goals you have at this specific time in your life. If you're looking for an ongoing relationship, accumulating notches may be detrimental for your goal since one-night meetings don't allow you to learn to handle real relationships. Even seasoned pick-up artists who have numerous notches may encounter that "special" girl and then end up acting as the character of a "simp" to earn the girl's affections.

The process of collecting notches helps you become an "sprinter." It's all about saying the things you have to say in the present to get relaxed. In contrast, lasting relationships can be described as "marathons." An excellent sprinter won't be a successful marathoner. Therefore, prior to deciding to accumulate notches, consider what you would like to achieve.

The red pill's goal is getting rid of the myths and myths we're required to accept about our world, and realizing that things are what they truly are. This isn't about forcing kids to what is known as the "pick up" or "hit it, then quit" style of life.

The red pill has been being compared to sleazy musicians due to their vocals tending to be the most loud (and the voices are frequently magnified by critics of drug). However, there is nothing wrong when it comes to collecting notches since the current culture is one where women can be smug collecting notches, so why should men not too?

It is crucial to remember that throughout all this, don't forget about your primary relationships goals.

Blue Pill Take

It is acceptable for people to have a sexual encounter in multiple relationships when they want to. However, men who seek for vulnerable women, presenting falsely their own sexuality, or sleeping with them in order that they can boast about it their acquaintances is a travesty. Some feminists want the entire society to begin identifying those who are sexy on false pretenses as sexual predators.

Blue pills are blue. The idea is that if intend to take notches, it is important to be honest and transparent about what you are planning to do with every woman who you sleep with so that you don't commit something that could be considered sexual attack.

Apart from that Blue pill movement can be described as generous about collecting notches. The blue pill movement even suggests having sexual encounters with as many people as you like, and the benefits include the fact that it helps you become better when it comes to sexual intimacy and makes your life more fun, and it's less exhausting than sleeping in a single bed It removes any ulterior motives out of the equation, as well as providing anxiety relief.

It also aims to encourage women in catching up their male counterparts in taking down notches.

No BS Take

The blue and red pill groups don't have a disagreement about whether it is appropriate to have regular sex whenever they are able to. It appears that the sole disagreement in their views is who should have the ultimate authority over sexual choices, and who is responsible for any emotional burdens that arise after informal sexual encounters. As a result, there is an absurd situation, where everybody is looking to have the time of their lives, and nobody is willing to pay for having fun. This is the generation that's not interested in consequence (just the observation of others, not judgement).

The majority of men want to enjoy informal sex with as many females as they can. However, they wouldn't like to wind having a romantic relationship with one who has several sexual relationships. Women would like to be on the game the same way that women do. But they don't want any of the men that they will end up having to consider that in their choice to be with they, irrespective of how much emotional baggage they acquire through the casual relationships. This is the real scenario on a global level.

You aren't everyone You are only you. Therefore, you need to adhere to your own personal principles in this case.

If you're looking to accumulate notches, it's an individual option. If you're a male living in a society of men there is a good chance that you'll be penalized for this selection.

But, prior to deciding to go through with it be aware the price, which you could have to pay for without knowing it. This will impact how you perceive women. It affects the way you view your self through the lens of the Judeo-Christian beliefs that likely shaped your upbringing. This can affect the way you allocate your funds and the way you establish the priorities for your lifestyle. This will affect the course of your personal life and the goals you set regarding your future. If you do manage to tear an individual down this could affect the structure and foundations of your next family.

It is your choice which option to take. about collecting notches. But do not follow the crowds who believe that it is possible to do so and not pay a penny for it. Determine what cost is and decide if you would be willing to pay for this amount.

If a woman has made the bet with her life, and you're not already, she'll carry a lot of luggage at the time you get to meet. Be aware of how much weight that burden is before you agree to with it. Be aware of what you're doing.

Chapter 5: Should I Put Women On A Pedestal?

Red Pill Take

Pedestalization is an extremely serious issue for beta males. It's the deliberate or unconscious desire to assign magic to beautiful women and even the men who are top of the line that you meet. If we set someone up in a position of authority and ignore imperfections and bad actions, and take responsibility for all which goes wrong in the interactions we have with their.

Pedestalization is a result of evolutionary, cultural and spiritual roots, in which we have a tendency to look at certain people believing that they are superior to others and even us. As a result of these fundamental factors even those who've seen the street have the ability to meet a woman who they decide is "the perfect one" then turn into foolishness or stalkers.

In order to avoid being a pedestal it is necessary to question the assumptions you have about someone. If you knock the woman off of a platform, the aura of magic that surrounds her will fade away and you'll be able to be able to see her as an imperfect real person. As a result, it will be easier to establish a rapport with her.

The red pill is a reminder that in order to progress women, you need to not do things which she didn't earn or isn't worthy of. If you continue to shower her with presents and affection her attention and affection, she'll start to think you are a petty person and will eventually drop out.

In all relationships it is necessary to have the alpha as well as the beta. When it comes to a functioning relationship between a man and woman, the male must be the alpha and the woman has to be the beta. No matter what she may say that she does not want to play the role of being the Alpha within the marriage. If she's forced into the role of an alpha, she'll rapidly lose the attraction that she feels for the guy. This is the way women are wired.

For their part, women are prone to place the person they're with in an unattainable pedestal. In order to be successful in a relationship, the man has to behave as if they are already sitting on the top of a pedestal. Also the man must strive to be his pedestal image which is in her mind. In most cases, the woman is likely to mention what she is expecting. If the man fails to meet the expectation, he's thrown out.

Blue Pill Take

Blue pill's approach to pedestalization usually addresses the issue of women placing men on pedestals but not the other way the other way around. Certain blue pill believers consider that, since the aim is equality that pedestalization should be avoided regardless of who is pedestalizing whom.

But, some who are in more mainstream circles (especially feminists) think that men are obligated to women to place their bodies on pedestals. women are no exception. If you're female and do not think that your spouse places you on the pedestal, that means he's not loving your as much as you would like him to.

The blue pill it is not just about friendships, and can affect people of all walks of their lives, from their work, relationships as well as what they think of their lives on a daily basis.

Certain psychologists suggest that pedestalization isn't inherent in the human condition, but it's the result of the individual's fears or feelings of attachment to another.

Self-defeating since it reduces the power of your "personal self-expression." It causes you to think that you're not a worthy person to be an unwavering, self-sacrificing person the person who you admire.

In order to combat the problem of being a pedestalized person, blue pills advise doing a consistent job of improving your self-esteem and overcoming the fears of being rejected.

No BS Take

The problem with putting people high on the pedestal is that you set the stage for them to fail or at the very least, to your own eyes. We have been conditioned to accept the notion that idolization does not exist in the way that both red pills and blue pills perceive it.

There is a possibility that it could be as a way to defend against rejection. If someone's "perfect" and rejects your application, then it's likely that you were denied by an angelic goddess and not a normal human being. So it's not a reason to feel bad over this. If they are "out from your realm," then just having taken the field for even a second should count as a success.

If you're in a relationship with someone, and make them feel like they're on the top of the world You can easily convince yourself that you're doing this because they're exceptional. However, in actuality the likelihood is that you're doing it in order to convince them that there is no other person who can give them the same respect as you do.

I'm not sure that, as human beings, we're in a position to miss the flaws of someone else. Humans are a highly intelligent species to face this kind of situation. It seems that we are able to see the flaws of others however we tend to dismiss them in exchange to gain something else.

If you place someone on the pedestal, a reason is your appreciation for them that you're trying to gain from the experience. Although you may believe you are unique you want to get them to choose you in comparison to others based on the way they interact with the person you are.

If you think about this from a perspective for resolving the issue of pedestalization one must realize that there is something in the human condition People are not satisfied with the services they receive. In fact, they are the beneficiaries of those favors. If you offer an individual a million dollars seemingly out from nowhere, they'll"thank you" and create tales in their heads of what they accomplish to be able to receive the money you gave them.

The saying goes that everybody has to be the hero of your own imagination. At the end of the day, whatever you go out of your manner to give to an individual girl is described as an act of merit.

The most important thing is that regardless of the way you see it, you stand an advantage with women if you do not place her on an unattainable pedestal. It is a common inclination to present people with gifts that are not worthy or statuses is usually defeating yourself. It is imperative to fight this urge with all the force you can. If you're around her, be aware of things that characterize her as human, such as the awkwardness of her, her flaws. Any sign that says it's just another individual, not any more or less than you are.

Chapter 6: Are Dark Personality Traits Such As Narcissism

Red Pill Take

Dark personality traits can be double-edged weapons when it comes to being successful with women both in relationship, both short and long-term. These traits may help you but they could also make you feel less successful, based upon whether or not you can apply effectively in every meeting with females.

Individuals with dark features are likely to have the ability to manipulate naturally The result is that these skills can be very beneficial if you simply want to be a flirt. In the long run, manipulating someone for the long run is not likely be successful in establishing a lasting connection.

If you're a psychopath ability, you may want to take on a female, work out what she would like in a guy, and portray yourself in the exact person she wants. However things turn out, there's no shameful feelings or guilt holding your from pursuing your goals. The only thing you have to worry about is your apex predator.

If you're Machiavellian You can be successful in the field of pickup art because when you have an "the ends justify the means" mentality, you'll make every effort in order to obtain the results you desire. Your moves are carefully planned, and the victory is guaranteed.

If you're socially savage, you'll never be thinking about what others think of your character, you'll be able to "do what you want to do" and take what you want from women.

If you're an expert narcissist, then you'll possess a positive self-esteem, which means that no woman can be able to take advantage of the fact that you are a master narcissist. Additionally, you will not hesitate to flirt with the prettiest women as you think that you (and nobody other than you) have the right to be treated with respect.

If you are looking for long-lasting relations, the very first aspect to be aware of is possessing some negative traits could help you get to the front of the line with ladies because they're attracted by men who have an "dangerous" or "mysterious" aspect. It's an evolutionary process.

Additionally, many dark aspects are a way to assert your power within the relationships, which means you're less likely to have a girlfriend who is a complete jerk or loses attraction to you due to the fact that you're a jerk.

There are, however, some darker characteristics that could be detrimental particularly if poorly controlled. If, for instance, you're a narcissist it is possible that you will meet an intelligent woman that plays you with a fiddle. Narcissists enjoy having their egos pampered, and so the only thing a lady has to do is give her a lot of compliments. She could even make you eat from her hands.

The second major flaw of dark characteristics is that you're used to using shortcuts or getting things done your way and settling for less, you could be in a disadvantage when you get to know the right woman and try to create an honest God connection with her. Dark-colored people have a low score on things like conscientiousness, humility as well as observing boundaries in social interactions and boundaries, all of which are crucial to an enjoyable connection.

Red pills acknowledge the fact that dark tendencies can be quite dangerous if not adequately understood, controlled and controlled by the person who owns these traits. The people with dark characteristics (particularly psychopathy) are often the perpetrators of some of the most horrific crimes discovered by mankind.

If you are a dark person You must remain socially active and make sure that you don't turn "antihuman."

If you want to make your dark side work for your life, they must be nurtured just as all other skills that will aid in your getting laid. If you're a dark person it is important to be sure that you're the one driving the traits and that the other will be the one who is in reverse.

Blue Pill Take

Individuals with dark features tend to display an increased sense of self-worth at one side, but an inability to take into account their feelings of others at the opposite end. They also have a tendency to be manipulative. That makes them extremely risky Potential lovers (particularly women) need to be cautious to stay away from such individuals and should look out for warning signs in the early stages of any new relationship.

People who have dark characteristics usually make good first impressions. This is because they appear attractive, cheerful and cocky. This is why women are often drawn to these guys, only to discover who they're dealing with only after it's been too long. Females are instructed to be cautious with those who are too prone to flattery and are known to make big gestures or extravagant promises in the beginning of relationships. People who the love too quickly and too much are particularly susceptible to these types of men.

A few mainstream psychologists have carried out studies that show that people with dark tendencies are often "selfish love partners" who do not pay attention to their partner and their needs. They may also resort to methods of coercion and manipulation to extract sexual pleasure from their partner.

It is recommended to stay clear of males who joke that are based on flimsy assumptions, engage in disapproving and gaslighting tactics to deny their position or show no compassion, or are overly obsessed with speaking about their own lives.

Particularly, dating apps are regarded as "platforms with a high level of" by men who are with dark characteristics. This is because the majority of these guys appear as smug and superficial both to them and with women they are pursuing.

No BS Take

A majority of what we consider "personality characteristics" are present throughout the world to various degrees. If it's not explicitly recognized as a disorder character trait is simply an observable behavior on a regular basis by someone else but not for other individuals. In most cases this is due to the individual's own experiences in contrast to something that is inherent to them.

If you had parents that made the impression that you are a prince constantly time It is likely that you had the impression that your worth was higher than others, and as consequently, you've got an egocentric tendancy.

If you have been through an professional, academic or setting, it is likely that you were taught to win regardless of cost So, congratulations! You are a Machiavellian.

If no one gave you the things you desired at the time you needed it and you have learned to pull on people's hearts to force them to grant the opportunity Congratulations, you're manipulative. This could make you sociopaths, or other depending on the manipulative techniques you use.

While the term "psychopathy" is often used in a casual manner, the concept of psychopathy is an entirely different subject, and we'll never dive into the subject. What's important is that those traits are common to the majority of everyone however the reason you have a particular trait could be the result of circumstances.

The field of psychology is social science. It is founded not on exact formulas but rather on an array of different people with opinions. If a large number of people are in agreement on something, then it is our duty to accept it as a the scientific truth.

Social scientists are required to study everything, categorize the information into clever categories and place a nice, neat name to it, so they appear to be genuine science. It's known as the physics envy. This is the method used by the researchers who came up with the so-called dark characteristics.

This means that everyone talks about the dark side of people, and human behavior is now a cause. When a man who isn't in good shape hits upon a female or a woman, they could be called an narcissist because he is out of his level. An attractive and fit man could also be labelled the narcissist who cares excessively about how he looks.

There are some who seem to be arrogant or malign, and in most instances, it's easy to spot. As we've seen before, human beings are intelligent enough to recognize flaws in their fellows but they don't acknowledge the flaws they see because they believe they can make a fair bargain.

Women have a keen sense of smell and are able to spot danger from afar. Yet, they're being manipulated by men who are malicious because there's a section of them who sees the malice as an advantage for evolutionary reasons when it comes to a possible partner. Manipulative man = manipulative offspring, which is a guarantee of the survival of.

We'd agree with the red pill on one point. As a guy and you feel you have a sense of darkness inside you, you must to know what it is, describe the concept in your own words as well as ensure you're in control of your behavior when you interact with others.

Furthermore the use of dark-trait techniques could be considered as looking to win or deceiving an individual. This can be beneficial for a single interaction but is self-destructive when you're attempting to develop relationships over time with someone. There is no way to go around by sabotaging your spouse or partner or bribing your partner into actions that are beneficial to you, but hurt the relationship. In the role of a teammate, the weakness of your partner becomes yours as well.

If you can manipulate someone to becoming detached from reality, you yourself are losing your own reality the process. If you make your spouse gaslight and make them dependent on her as you'll start to demand certain things from her that nobody other person with a rational mind would ever be able to give. If she does finally walk off of you (and believe me when I say that, considering the way our society has advanced, changed, she'll) You will then find yourself alone and within a prison mental made by you.

However, whatever that you do to earn an individual's affection is technically considered to be manipulative. Where should be your moral benchmark?

The best standard to go with is to ask yourself. "Is this malicious, and can be harmful to her?" If not, this unjustified feeling of self-importance, the silver tongue, the ability to twist any tale in order to claim yourself as the person to be, might just be the thing you require to convince your spouse to pay attention to you.

Chapter 7: Should I Be Concerned About A Woman's Sexual History?

Red Pill Take

In this regard the movement known as the red pill includes catchy words that the majority might consider to be outright sexist. It is said that "today's woman is the prostitute of yesterday" as well as "all women have the hoe-phrase" warning young men to look out at women who appear as "good women," when in fact the reality is that they were spending their early times sleeping with a slew of men who were shady.

The movement known as the red pill has two opposing schools of thought concerning how men must confront this dilemma. The second school of thought believes men to set real expectations of women and not view women as Disney princesses, but instead as genuine people with innate an instinct that is as animalistic just like men's.

The school of thought that this is based on suggests men take to the streets and grab the attention of promiscuous women to ensure that they do not feel deprived or angry as they age and are looking to be settled.

The other school of thought concentrates on younger men seeking to be sexy however, rather those who seek long-lasting relationships. The advice is to steer clear of those who have "wasted their time" and are no longer regarded to be "wife of the future."

The majority of them believe that men ought to research the history of a woman's sexuality (from sources that aren't her personal word of mouth) prior to deciding whether or not to engage in an ongoing relationship with her. According to them, this is due to the fact that learning shocking information regarding a person with whom you've put much trust could cause irreparable harm.

On forums for red pills, certain men discuss "horror" warning tales of sexually arousing women who go as in the direction of moving into different states, cities and even countries to avoid their sexual fantasies and "trap" an unsuspecting good man.

Blue Pill Take

Based on"the blue pill," if have a problem with the sexuality of your partner and you are unable to resolve it, two people have responsible - yourself and the society. It is you who are the most guilty for having trouble letting go of the resentments that society has imposed upon you.

The society has a myriad of guidelines for the way women behave even though the majority of these guidelines are no longer relevant but their traces are still around. That's the reason many men think that they are the ones who own women's past. In addition to religion "traditional beliefs" the society teaches males to control in regards to female sexuality. This is simply not right.

This movement encourages those who believe that women's sexual experiences are against themselves, to think about an instance wherein women decide to put his absence of sexual experiences against him.

According to surveys, the majority of women stated that, should they were confronted by their spouse about the sexual history of their partner as a negative experience, it would come to a stop until they were offered a genuine apology as well as a guarantee that such an infuriating statement will never be mentioned in the future.

In the case of the blue pill there is a clear line the fact that nothing you did prior to the time you became an official item is something men are allowed to be a critic over. Any man who wants to investigate the past of a woman is deemed "controlling" and alone is an indication of trouble.

The blue pill analyzes the issue using the perspective of equality. According to them, it's morally wrong to highlight the female sexuality if it is more acceptable for males. The majority of women don't hold a male's past sexuality against him. To be fair, males should not do the same.

There is no need to be a snarky comment. The subject of the past sexual experience triggers more thoughts than many other subjects that are discussed in relationships and dating. In general, people wish their sexual past to be seen by others positively (heroic and prudent, typical given one's age, etc.) rather than negative terms (inadequate or excessive and so on.). It is a broader issue for men and women.

Women will often describe a female who's had more sexual encounters than she has as the word "slut," but for all the world she'll never even imagine herself to be an individual. Everybody wants to be considered good-hearted, and no one wants to hear someone say that they're not.

Sexual history can be a painful issue for young men who face a tough time persuading females to sleep with their. That is why, once you learn "her number" it's hard not to look at it in comparison to the one you have.

If you're a guy who's angry about an ex-girlfriend's sexuality It's probable that were you given the same opportunities to sleep in a bed as she did, you'd have sought out every one. This is the real cause of anger, as well as the reason why you feel like you've been cheated.

Based on our current social norms There is an unanimity that anyone is entitled to be out to sleep in the company of as many other people as they wish Instead of being viewed as sexually attractive, they'll instead be considered "virile" individuals with a desire to "celebrate" the sexual pleasures of their lives.

The difference (in the quantity of partners) is due to the nature of women being followed, and men do the following. Anyone who's attractive enough knows that guys were pursuing her at the very least since her teenage years. Therefore, the men who dated her were always there for her. She did not have to visit her, and always could pick her own.

The side has to go by himself. He has learn how to play and package himself. He must also make his moves, and then get knocked down more often than otherwise.

Imagine two individuals meeting following numerous years of having these encounters, and looking at each other as potential partners. Then there's the scoreboard.

In this instance she looks back at her past sexuality and thinks that she's done her best to stay cautious. On his own, is looking at her past sexual inclinations and among the many things they could possibly be, one thing stands out which irritates him: the truth that she (along along with the rest of the women) have said "yes" to every one of those males, but he was forced endure rejection after rejection to receive an occasionally "maybe." This is what causes anger.

So, what can men take to address this issue? As I mentioned earlier in this article, the focus does not lie on what's the best or most optimal, but rather focused on the practicable. If you're the type of person who is a caveman on this subject is what you're. If you don't acknowledge this, it's going to result in a great deal of unresolved pain. This could turn into a pervasive type of anger.

If you are aware, in your heart you're not able to live without a woman's history and you're not obligated to and the society shouldn't force you to. There is always another person with baggage is manageable to carry.

For the sake of factuality, we need to keep in mind that a woman's previous sexual past is not necessarily a sign of her behavior in the future. The "virtuous" lover can over time alter, and even transform to someone who you don't recognise. However someone who has an "sordid" background could become the most trustworthy person that you'll ever come across.

People are said to be able to alter their behaviour, however they are unable to change their habits. The instinct is the one we turn to when the chips are down.

We believe that this is where that the real issue is. If you're trying figure out if someone will be a cheater according to your "eventful" sexual behavior It could be helpful to identify if a majority of their decisions were based on instinct or just based on their behavior.

If something is done instinctively that is, it happens with no knowledge and in complete confidence. When we perform it as mere habitual behavior that we perform, it is done but with a few apprehensions. we won't be able to repeat it when given the opportunity.

If you've got an argument to believe that your spouse's behavior that was shared with several friends before was just in fact instinctual, and not just a matter of behavior and not just a matter of luck, enter into the partnership knowing that, given an opportunity, she'll be able be able to revert back to her fundamental instincts. Do you think this relationship is worthwhile to invest in?

If you're not living up to yourself and your partner is not being true to you, then the relationship is bound to be a failure. If you believe strongly in the importance of being prudent and so on you believe in, don't put yourself in an arrangement with people who don't align with your beliefs simply because you're told that's the right thing to do.

Chapter 8: Should I 'Simp?'

Red Pill Take

In general, the red pill tries to stay away from ridiculing men's negative behavior towards women rather, they try to "educate" these men to be more open-minded in order to win with women.

Simps are the sole exception. In the eyes of the red pill, they are deserved to be ridiculed since unlike beta males they have a softer stance to women, knowingly and through decision. Simps can possess all of the physical characteristics associated with an alpha male, yet he chooses to act more obnoxious as the weakest beta.

The source of the term simp has been debated. It is believed that it's the abbreviated version from "simpleton," while others believe it's the exact opposite from "pimp." However, in any situation, the meaning is clear and is a staple of the world of today's culture.

If someone calls another person simps, the implication is evident - that he will go the extra mile to do favors for a lady in the hopes to be noticed by her out of a crowded group of men who are doing the similar thing.

The most common scenario is of protecting a woman who's not your partner from legitimate comments from men who aren't yours or taking an unbiased female viewpoint during the "battle of the genders" debate, and the most damaging of all, spending money with a woman that whom you're sexually attracted to but you're not receiving any profit from the investment.

In the event that a simp is not a distinct part of the group of men who are who are interested in the same woman the simp is often referred to in the context of an "orbiter." These pills dislike simps and orbiters due to their perception of them as hypocrites.

They try to portray their self as cool guys that care for the woman they are interested in However they have goals that are similar to those of all men. What they've got is nothing more than an unproductive sexual plan since every male who lacks conviction and imagination does exactly the same thing as they're doing.

To make it more hilarious for the simp, a lot of women have realized their vulnerability and they're exploiting them in a mass way. "E-girls," "instathots," as well as other savvy women are curating their internet material specifically for the egos of simps, so that they will continue to milk their stupid thighs to the fullest extent possible.

It's simple to spot an online simp however, according to"the Red Pill," a lot of people are caught smuggling in their lives and don't even realize that they are doing it.

As an example, suppose you're in a circle that includes a number of guys with only one female and even though you are in relationship with her, but one of your friends gives the gift to her but they aren't the one, then you're a fool. You're a side figure, perhaps simply a prop for the film of her life. You isn't even far from being the most prominent male. Make your own movie.

If you believe that you're forming bonds with another girl due to something that's popular rather than something that is significant, then you're an obnoxious scum. If you're watching the same show on TV or listen to the similar music or play the exact same video games with an individual, it means very little. Pop culture is called that for an reason. Millions of people enjoy the same thing, and don't jog about thinking that it makes you more attractive to the woman you're with. It's more important to have a personal connection than that, and the relationship must be mutual.

When you're going out for your "group hangs" you find her constantly laughing at another man's jokes then this is who she's with. It's not that you aren't attentive to her however, it's someone else who is laughing at her. Red flag big.

Then, last but not the least, is when she's always talking about her problems with men who aren't yours and you don't know why - STOP! It's all emotional nonsense. Don't believe you're special since you're the one who is trusted.

For those who take the red pill (and in some cases, even women) the simp is viewed as unassuming creeps. They choose to "invest" their time and energy into relationships with other people (the woman) without their knowledge or permission. This is referred to as the "covert contract" in which one may feel as if he's owed sexual gratification or a connection due to the things he's done to a woman but the woman was never a part of the exchange in the first instance.

To red pills, calling out simps can be an effective way to protect women from scumbags that disguise as gentlemen. Ladies, you are very welcome.

Blue Pill Take

If the blue pill were to be allowed they'd completely eliminate simp as a popular lingua franca. Indeed, they've tried so many times. Major publications have written thought essays on why "simp behavior" is sexist, and certain technology platforms have blocked remarks that use the term. Men's magazines, too, have said that men who criticize "simp behaviour" on other males as "messed down, entitled slobs."

Blue pills have attempted to change the "simp" description to a strawman defense. In particular, they've stated that men could be called simps simply for complimenting women.

The purpose of this the program, according to them, is using peer pressure to squelch any respect men feel in regard to women. From this perspective the word simp can be consequently deemed offensive, demeaning and antifeminist.

Blue pills have been formulated with tips about what "good boys" who are referred to as simps by their peers could be taught to use the term "as an emblem of respect." The teenage males and boys are urged to not feel ashamed of being considered simps since they're following the "right way" in the way they behave towards women. The society, according to them, will reward these men for their good conduct.

There have been numerous reports that teenage boys are described as simps by friends Their mothers are forced sent the boys to therapy due to being harassed. According to the blue pill, it's a sexual orientation that should be eradicated before it can spread to the future generation.

No BS Take

The people who string each other around emotionally. As men pursue each other so it is only natural that you will see them strung far more often as women.

Women are known to are able to manipulate men in a bid to make a point or achieve the intention of gaining self-esteem. The particular type of woman is both incentivized as well as increased via the internet as well as social media. That is the reason why they've become easily identifiable. But, they've always existed, and have always left behind a trail of heartbroken and broken males in their wake.

It is important for men to recognize the signs of a woman and steer clear of them like the women they eat. In our study, we'll examine the relationship dynamics of two people who have known one another personally, and not one who is in love with an online celebrity.

Women who are the majority that bind men aren't doing it for malicious motives. The reason they do it is that first they wish to be loved.

The majority of cultures believe that women are taught to appear "nice," so even the time they'd like to reject a man (especially ones that they have in common friendship circles) and they don't say no but will allow room to "friendship," keeping in the mind that they'll still have to make friends with their partner.

Due to their narrow vision in pursuing females, men are either unable to see this or think of it as an opportunity to put down the foundation for another shot. This is often the time when simping takes on the fullest intensity.

Imagine you're a man who has a relationship with a girl. It is obvious that she is lovely. You believe she's special and maybe she's "the the one." What should you do?

I guarantee you that your initial response will be to flirt. If you continue to do "friend activities" to her it'll keep you on the lookout to win her affections. You start with little things, like buy her coffee, take the boxes up the stairs.

If you keep doing that you do it, the more relaxed she becomes soliciting favors from you, and the more inclined to accept these favors (because it seems like you're getting better). After a while, down the period, you find out that you're an all-fledged addict, and that you are unable to say "no" in response to her demands is "out from the norm." It's like you're an addict as well as a victim.

It is perfectly fine building a relationship with a lady so that you get another opportunity to talk to her. But, be extremely cautious when you go about it since you could be in chance of getting caught in the rabbit hole of simping.

If you are in the simping rabbit hole You are most likely to be in the following situations, as well as other similar situations:

It's getting late, she's stuck at a event you were not invited to and you're the one who she asks for help but you don't get anything from it, other that another "great man" Gold star.

The woman keeps calling you in terms of "boyfriend material" or "husband material" however she is constantly turning her back and seeking relationships with men.

The girl flirts with males when you are around.

You are "defending her honour" against those whom they themselves keep inviting to her home.

The woman that decides on where you go together or what you're doing.

If you are taking pictures of her (if she allows it) You are that person who is leaning in her direction but her attitude is typically nonchalant.

In regards to guys accusing other men of being pimps, in the first place let me say that you should not make your own judgments about your own opinions on strangers on the web. Most of them are people who will say whatever they want to get them off.

If a trusted person, or even a man who you consider to be decent or even goes out of their ways to suggest or claim that you're the type of person who is a smuggler, then you need to be aware. You might have a suspicion that he is thinking something that you're not.

My experience is that males between the ages of 17 and over don't have any qualms in sharing tips for relationships. If a friend of yours tells you that you're doing too many things for her do not believe his words. it.

A key factor to avoid becoming a slouch is to keep your own agenda in the forefront. Always keep engaged in your job, work or any other pursuits and make sure you have priority over your partner's.

If you're spending much of your time with a lady who you love consider what benefits you're getting out of this. The answer isn't the fact that you're investing into the possibility of a future romance. If having her within your business all time will help you connect with new women or raising the profile of possible partners (because having her around attracts them) It could be worth the investment. Make sure you don't tell yourself lies.

Don't go around telling yourself that you are hanging out with a girl because you are her friend, yet, whenever a random guy walks over and hits on her in your company, you feel crushed, jealous, and start reacting passive-aggressively. Be a bit more shrewd.

If you find yourself contemplating "I do not see what she thinks of that man, he's not bad for her and I'm far superior to him" Then you dig to your purse and make a purchase for the next time she drinks - You're a shopper!

Chapter 9: How Do I Handle The Fear Of Rejection?

Red Pill Take

For those who take red pills, rejection is an aspect of being a male. Even the most beautiful and athletic, wealthy and confident males receive rejection from women every single time. If you're having a hard time with rejection What makes you believe you're unique?

It is normal to be disqualified by females hundreds, or even thousands of times in your lifetime. It's impossible doing anything about it, and it is better to prepare your thoughts for the possibility of rejection (the being out there and asking for it) rather than feigning fear from fear.

Certain red pill aficionados recommend young men take to the streets and meet all women that they can and pile the most rejections can be in order to shield their bodies from the anxiety of being rejected.

For them, the most effective method to deal with the rejection process is to break outside of your comfort space. Always seek out women regardless of whether you feel as though you're being a jerk. If, for instance, you're passing by an establishment and see someone you would like to have an evening with or hang outside, the blue pills will urge you to act immediately. Go into the establishment, visit her, and then ask for her number, no matter the skepticism you may think it is. The fear of being rejected makes you seek out perfect relationships which don't happen in actual everyday life.

It is important to face rejection in a calm, steady manner. If you behave like you're a fuckup when faced with rejection, then even the woman will know you took the right decision.

The Red Pills also suggest that take the direct approach when dealing with females and accept the rejection as men would. Instead of taking the indirect method for a means of defending the risk of a severe rejection but only to find yourself in the "friend zone" because you didn't fully communicate about your motives right from the beginning.

It's more appropriate to take a girl out for a drink and be rejected, rather than asking her contact number and "playing the game slowly" in the process prolonging the pain you're suffering from, simply because you'd like her to respond "no" in front of you.

If you continue to pile on your rejections, you could become an "approaching machine." Every girl won't appear "too cute" to meet, and you'll never miss your opportunity to get in touch with any girl you meet at some point in the future.

Unexperienced men often imagine being disapproved of by women as a loss, but the red pill can tell the fact that you took actions and improved your resilience during this process makes your whole experience successful.

There are a lot of guys around who look good and are considered to be appealing to women. But they don't know since they've never approached women because they fear rejection. Actually, a lot of males who take a trip to "pile rejects" will be surprised that the vast majority of the handful of women they approach will actually agree to it.

"Ask for it and it will be given to you." It's taken from the Bible the Bible itself. A fear of rejection stops the person from asking. And is it possible to have something when you haven't asked to receive it?

Blue Pill Take

The blue pill concentrates upon what a man needs to do to be respectful to a woman and allow her to be free when she is rejected, but less on the way a man can handle this rejection in terms of his personal emotional state. However, it does offer some concepts worth learning on if you're male.

The first thing to remember is that one should not accept rejection as a personal attack. They say that"the "it's not you I'm the one who's being rejected" phrase is an old fashioned one. If someone doesn't like you It's their fault, not about you. Perhaps their lives are crammed in the present. They may be struggling emotions for an individual. They might feel they aren't compatible. Perhaps you don't meet the mental list they've created to help them find a partner.

However, the fact that the person who isn't liking your appearance isn't a reflection of how attractive you appear to others and you shouldn't consider it a personal attack.

It sounds great, however it becomes a little too preachy after that. When you're not taking it personal, as per blue pills, those who are the one who was rejected are required to treat the woman. Be aware that it's very difficult to refuse someone. People are naturally drawn to being loved, and to say no to someone could be the most damaging way in order to get them off of the person. Therefore, whether you do not be fooled it took some courage to get that woman not to tell you no.

Kindness is the key, so take away the pain and shame. A desire to harm someone who has injured you can be a damaging force (not only to you but also towards you) So if you allow it to win it, both of you suffer. Simply say something along line of "I am sorry," and take your off.

You're perfectly fine to are feeling hurt. But keep in mind that it's not your blame. The majority of pain shouldn't be blamed on a person Certain pains may be chronic pains. If you feel it's all your fault, then the idea is that you've committed a mistake, however it's not true. You, too, haven't committed any wrongdoing by refusing to accept you. The only thing that matters is how it is.

Blue pills advise you to keep a away from those who have rejected you, at the very least, for a time. If you're in a close relationship (i.e. do you have colleagues, or move into the same social circle) staying away from each other for a time could prove advantageous for both of you. For this reason it is possible to keep yourself active to alleviate your desire to be attentive. This can also assist in getting her off your thoughts.

No BS Take

It isn't obvious that women will not like her until she is rejected by you. The hesitation to admit in asking her to date can be more destructive than rejection by itself due to the fact that it's self-rejection.

However, even that knowledge won't ease the anxiety and anxiety that you experience when you think about whether or not to ask a girl out. The reason is that the worry of being rejected is deep in our brains. It is our nature in our biology to be part of a group (in couples or to social groups) which is why the notion of being turned down, rejected, isolated and vilified is a nightmare.

As with all forms of anxiety, it's once you're on the opposite side to realize just how insignificant the fear of rejection had been inside your brain. The only method to deal the fear is to take it on.

Therefore, the red pills say the only method to conquer the anxiety of being rejected is to be rejected. go through the experience, and realize that it wasn't nearly as catastrophic as you had hoped it could be.

It's a good idea to try rejection, particularly when it comes to situations with lower stakes before having to deal with the same situation with someone you've been carrying the torch for an extended time.

However, the other side of that side is that, If we're only thinking of the possibility of pain relief, it's best to reach out to someone you like and then be rejected in the early stages rather than being dismissed after having been deeply emotionally involved. The pain of rejection is less when there's not a lot of anticipation about their occurrence. An "no" from an uninvolved girl at an establishment isn't as damaging as one coming from the same woman if you've been messaging to and from her for a long time. In my experience, when I'm scared of the future, it's helpful to imagine the scenario that could happen within my mind, and then take it to absurdity, and then make fun of it

It's true that the most dangerous thing she can do would be "no." But the anxiety can cause you to believe that the answer will become the equivalent of "oh that's not right!" and the whole crowd will be laughing and make a point. Everyone who you attended school with will discover that you're going to need to relocate to a different location and alter your name. But everyone will instantly recognize your name as a member of"the "rejection registry" which they are on, and you'll be buried inside a cabin far from the forest, and your tombstone will say "here is the ultimate repeller for women" and the ghost of your virgin is going to roam the earth and be pursued by female ghost-busters.

Haha!

Forget about all that.

Whatever you're looking for There is only one method to go. Be sure to look at your best, go towards her, and ask to have a minute of her time and then make short and honest phrases, and then ask her to go on dates. Keep your distance, and do not to look foolish as you wait patiently for the "no." Once it comes, the definitive"no" is received, make sure to wish her a happy birthday, then take a walk (do not walk) away. This is all there is to this. If you do these instructions in a sloppy, Forest Gump sort of manner, you could shut off your brain to just do it. And, sometimes there's a chance that it won't necessarily be a "no."

Chapter 10: Are Traditionally Male Traits And Behaviors Toxic To Society?

Red Pill Take

The whole movement of the red pill was founded on one assumption the fact that there's an increase in the absence of positive masculinity within Western cultural. Men, as well as all masculine characteristics, are considered to be a backward, evil and "problems" which need to be resolved.

The Red Pills believe that as a result of an in-correction that is occurring as culture changes both boys and men are being disenfranchised, if not even discriminated against in the face of increasingly influential gatekeepers of the liberal wing of the culture. Red pill advocates for people to rethink any description of everyone as bad and think independently instead of adhering to what is being taught.

The red pill is a traditional way to treat masculine traits like aggression and aversion to feelings, attempting to appear physically and mentally robust, staying away from a relationship with men who are emotional insensitive and constantly trying to achieve self-sufficiency are not necessarily negative aspects. They are factors that have led to the human race has been able to endure and flourish all this time, and females are a welcomed addition.

It is becoming a common effort to eliminate these characteristics among boys in the earliest years, and this is detrimental in terms of the mental health of the kids themselves as well as for the society as a whole. In spite of what liberals keep talking on about gender stereotypes, they have a reason. There is a place for men to fulfill, and it is impossible for them to play the job if the tools that they require to get the job accomplished are deemed to be a demon by the society.

The characteristics that are thought to be harmful can actually be essential for manhood. Man must be assertive. What else can he do be able to provide to and secure his family (as his biological wiring is designed to)? He must abide by his stoic nature and keep his emotions in check. If not, who's likely to be the one who can provide courage and comfort for the entire family when every member of the family from the infant to the father is crying at the same time? Manhood is a must for any man. Are you the type of person who would be an older man simply because they cannot handle daily life's challenges?

Other "toxic" male characteristics (mental physical and mental toughness, emotional insensitivity and an laziness towards others) are viewed as essential for preparing the man particularly during his early years in order to be sufficiently prepared to accept the role of a man.

A few red pills have been so powerful as to say that if the stigmatization of masculine characteristics is not stopped, Western civilization might fall. This is because while males within the West are raised in the same way as girls, boys from different parts of the globe are being "raised correctly," so in the future, when men from elsewhere "come to fight us" along with their "real men" there will be just a few "girly guys" who are fighting for our cause and will be losing to our adversaries.

Also, the Red Pills claim that there's a disconnection between the changes to culture which are being imposed on both boys and men, and what society (especially women) is actually expecting from males. As an example, even though it is expected that children be taught to be emotionally tolerant however, the reality is that women do not want to live in a relationship with a man who "whines" on his feelings just as she would. This same principle applies to other acts of chivalry that women still expect from their male counterparts despite requiring an absolute equality on different fronts.

Blue Pill Take

To the blue pill, toxic masculinity is real and harmful to the society at large, and the need to eradicate it in all ways. The masculine stereotypes and social norms affect not only women but the society as a whole however, also men in their own right. In shaming harmful masculinity, the liberal community protects males from their own self-destructing ways. You're welcome, bro.

Men are dominant in society and have to be treated as such is an idea that is a "traditional stereotypical view" which has been responsible for a variety of homophobic violence, gender-based violence as well as wars, crimes, social inequity, and many other vices that men have come across.

The patriarchy continually perpetuates itself with its harmful ideas via logics like "boys will always be boys" "it's an issue for men," "man up," and "boys do not cry." If you ever are surrounded by people who say these phrases and you want to fight them, it is imperative that you challenge the patriarchy by putting these misconceptions straight.

At a very young age the boys are enticed into the male-dominated club of toxic masculinity because they are allowed to behave in a threatening manner and harass other children at the playground. In order to stop this from happening the boys must be taught to be as social as girls. This means that they should not engage in actions that can result in violence.

A tendency for men to repress their emotions and self-reliance can be harmful for them as it can lead to depression, insufficient communication and high stress levels and an increased likelihood of abusing substances as well as other psychological issues.

In order to deal with these issues To deal with these issues, children are expected to be able to vent their anger in every situation They should also not be able to dismiss or ignoring the feelings of others, as this encourages them to suppress their personal feelings.

The blue pill male norms can be harmful because of the messages they convey about feminine. If males are taught they are "unmanly" to share their emotions, this implies that women's desire to express themselves is the sign of vulnerability. This is why traditional masculinity is in essence, anti-feminist.

No BS Take

In every country both genders are traditionally divided into specific gender duties. If the gender roles weren't fulfilled family and community members wouldn't be in a position to function. With the changing of the society throughout the years, these duties have also changed along in line with changing times.

The expectations society has set for gender roles for men and women has maintained a fairly steady pace despite shifts in the gender roles triggered by education, industry as well as technological advancements. This isn't the result of chance, and surely isn't the result of a unilateral development of the patriarchy.

Our nature is the basis of culture but not the other reverse. It is impossible for culture to be anything but a negative reflection of the natural world. This is a thought-provoking exercise The time is late in the night and you and your partner are both in bed. The two of you alerted by an unusual alarming sound from the room next to you. The two of you exchanging glances. The one of you has to and look it up. What is the one it's going to be?

It is possible that she will go for a workout more frequently than you are (if you know which gym it is) and may be better than you, however in the event that she's police officers or something else and you're both aware when you glance at each other that it is you who needs to investigate. There's no doubt about that in your own mind, or the mind of her.

It's the role of male - to safeguard both you and your family. Our cavemen forefathers knew this but she's aware, and you are aware of it, as well. If you are apathetic now, good luck with the chances of ever reproduction.

In all cultures, both genders into certain role, and not in order to slash or control one gender however, to maximize the overall positive effects to society. What's the purpose of cultural heritage if it fails to benefit the society? The males were naturally skilled at some things. Women are naturally more adept in many other aspects. Therefore, our forefathers built their lives around those inherent skills. This is the same culture that we have inherited.

Everybody has a responsibility to fulfill. When it comes time arrives, everybody is obliged to play their the role. If you aren't able to, what is your contribution to society? Negating the existence or the importance of gender roles isn't going to bring you to a higher level of understanding, but it can make you appear self-righteous. You think that you are more knowledgeable than the hundreds of generations of our grandparents on the shoulders of whom you sit. While it's one thing to suggest additions to the roles you're playing, it's quite another way to eliminate them totally.

Sexuality is a part of males, but they also are passed down by the manner in which he is taught. If a child exhibits aggression, it is inherent to him. The best way to raise the boy's character isn't to make him be a victim, but rather is to help him transform that natural instinct to become an effective energy. This is why, in our culture the boys are taught to be respectful of women and not to ever hurt girls.

Society is already aware of how to manage boys' harmful traits, and then turn these traits into a force for good. The boys are taught how to manage their impulsiveness through competitive sports. They learn to develop their curiosity by participating in scouts and other teams. The drive to be self-sufficient is developed when they learn the life-skills. This is how it's supposed to function. This is how it's worked.

The argument can be made for the fact that gender roles have gone out of fashion, and the underlying manifestations of them harm society more than they aid the cause. It's not the same idea as claiming that the masculine characteristics are inherently harmful.

People who claim to fix the "masculinity issue" can actually make the problem worse. They just aren't aware of it. The responsibilities of a woman are clearly defined to her right from the beginning, men must be taken seriously. If not, he'll develop into an irritable blob with insatiable interest.

Every boy should be taught in a direct or indirect way "Do this, because it's what is expected of a man." If the world does not want to educate men on how to become men, it shouldn't be a complaint that there aren't any "real men" in the world.

Chapter 11: Are Video Games, Porn, Sports, And Social Media Bad For You?

Red Pill Take

The red pill movement to the red pill movement, pornography watching and video games, watching the latest sports and scrolling social media sites are detrimental for you development as a male. The majority of "modern males" are addicted to these kinds of things which is the problem nobody is discussing.

The "vices could appear distinct, but at their base, they're alike in that they keep youngsters from self-actualizing. The act of engaging in these vices creates individuals a false sense fulfillment or satisfaction.

When you binge watch pornographic films and you masturbate, the brain will be satisfied in the exact manner as it would have been had you sex with real girls.

If you are a gamer and you kill zombie Nazis or something else it is satisfying to know that you've accomplished some physical exercise, but it is actually that you simply sat on your couch for the entire day.

When you browse through social media, and you read other the posts of people who aren't so clever Your brain is satiated like you've discovered new information that is useful and interesting.

If you are a fan of sporting events, your brain gets happy thinking that you're winning, but reality is that you're only living in the vicariously of the athletes doing their best every day, earning money, and actually winning.

In the meantime, you exercise to not be active, your muscles weaken, you gain weight And then you ask what is wrong with your life.

The pleasures of these addictions creates the beta male. Instead of doing your thing, you're in your home just watching your friends live the life Your brain consequently, believes that people are more successful than the you.

While watching pornography generally the thing you're doing is watching a man having sex with another girl, and you're going away with the sex. Although you may not be aware of it however, you're actually creating self-esteem by watching an uninformed.

The trend to watch streamers playing video games could be more harmful than actually playing the games by yourself if you use similar logic. You basically agree to suck at something sucky until you are having someone else play it for you.

While scrolling on social media, you're looking at other users who are dating hot women and lead exciting lives while you're sitting there. This can hurt your self-esteem, and puts these people more attractive than you in your head.

It's the same for watching the sports. They are people in great fitness doing things they can't do. It's time to go out and enjoy some basketball rather than watching larger strong men slamming the ball. It's the greatest option for your self-esteem.

And then there's the problem of time. Are you aware of what time you devote to these addictions?

It's quite easy for men to begin porn when he goes up, believing it'll only take some minutes. He'll after a while, find that he's continuing to watch it even though it's time to be sleeping. It affects his capacity to be productive throughout the day and achieve his goals in life and engage in regular physical exercise.

When you're playing online games, it's difficult to keep track of time which means time off from work, sleep study, forming friendships, and many more essential aspects.

If you are a fan of the sport the games usually consume large chunks of time that you will never return. That's not even getting into betting on sports and fantasy.

Social media can be a terrible time consumeer because it's constantly present, and is continually being upgraded. Additionally, it can be addictive as it can be difficult to stay away from your work in search of that itching by clicking refresh to check if there's fresh posts that are interesting.

It's rare to come across men who aren't dependent on at least one of these substances. A lot of men waste lots of time or energy, their capacities of the brain, as well as "valuable seed" but they gain very little from it, apart from poor self-esteem and personality flaws. It's difficult to concentrate on the development of their lives due to being continuously distracted. They do not even know the amount of time they're wasting.

The pill is a red one that encourages people to become better by putting an effort to rid themselves from these addictions. They provide a lot of tips about how to "taper off" or "quit completely cold turkey."

Blue Pill Take

The Blue Pill movement generally is dismissive of the use of video games, pornography and sports viewing, as well as other social media-related scrolling. However, in rare instances when they spot a potential negative effect on individuals, the pressure to make changes is put not at the level of an individual however, on a particular segment or group of people e.g. the education system, large technology, or even the patriarchy.

In the case of pornography The blue pill believes that there's nothing fundamentally incorrect with the consumption of such content. It also insists that children must be taught what to do when they encounter the material. It's not the fact that children watch porn. The problem is because there's such a huge negative stigma surrounding porn that there is no system put in place to help youngsters to distinguish the difference between entertainment and the real world. The solution is to ensure that the spectrum of sex education needs to be increased to ensure that children are educated about pornography at schools.

Not focusing on the issue of youth According to"the blue pill," can be useful in a variety of ways. It is, for instance, an opportunity to learn about different things as well as discover different sexual "interests." Also, it's an ideal tool for examining other sexual identities as well as to determine if you're different from the gender that society imposes upon the people around you (this is especially important for those who live within an area of "repressed" society).

People who feel that their self-esteem has been negatively affected by the exposure to porn are urged to consume less "body positive" material which "represents the person they are." On the other hand the men should not insist that their partner do what they watch in porn films. They should also stay from "misogynistic videos," a term used to describe adult content in which men show a the most dominance over females.

If it's gaming and sporting events, blue pills adhere to the "to every one their own" principle. If you enjoy these kinds of sports, "you do you," and nobody else can call your a lazy person.

There are millions of gamers who make money by playing games on the internet and streaming and games, which makes it possible to make a career of it for those who enjoy it. If you do not like these kinds of activities people call you the "boomer," an old individual with an unjustified sense of superiority morally. Furthermore, certain games are considered sporting events, so you're in the right place.

In the case of the social web, blue pills are in agreement with the red pill that using excessive amounts of it could negative affect your self-esteem and lower your performance.

There is a difference in assignment of blame and accountability. For the blue pills the big tech companies have the responsibility to ensure that the content we view on social networks isn't affecting the health of our minds and bodies. Zuckerberg has to create a fresh filter that will ensure that the pictures of gorgeous Instagram models won't cause teenage girls feel uncomfortable regarding their body.

In the same way of solving problems in technology through technological solutions In the event that apps that are on your smartphone distract you all the time you can download other apps you can install to reduce interruptions caused by the initial collection of apps.

No BS Take

These activities (watching porn, sports or porn and wasting time playing social media and playing video games) are merely forms of escape.

Escapism is the act of escaping away from a particular aspect of your life which you consider boring uncomfortable, hard, or difficult. Escapisms typically take shape of either entertainment (externally) as well as the imagination (internally).

Other types of escape (besides those that we've been discussing within this section) are contemplating the day and viewing "informative" YouTube clips drinking, using alcohol and drugs, stuffeding one's faces (overeating) and, intriguingly, sinking oneself within the job.

This last instance should prove you that different types of escapism have advantages. When you're absorbed within your job to get away from your relationship that is failing It could be said as a good thing.

When looking at your experience is it a mistake when you judge it based upon its advantages and disadvantages. Instead, consider it through the perspective of the opportunity cost.

In the case of escapism it is important to know what you ought to be doing in this moment, but you're taking care of. It's what you're loss. In the event that, for example, you're supposed to be seeking a job but your engaging in video gaming instead, then you're missing the chance of a stable job.

Escapisms can be self-repetuating. This means that when you are involved with them, the chances of engaging again are greater. These can be said to be addictive and this increases the risk. It is easy for them to turn into harmful behaviors as each time you indulge it becomes harder to break and even more difficult.

The four escapisms that are criticized by red pills are perverse because they possess an attribute that other types of escapism do not have: they are able to replicate the reality.

Drinking alcohol may help your escape for a while but it does not provide you with a feeling of achievement. These four types of escapisms are extremely risky because apart from giving you leave, they can create a feeling that you've achieved an important goal that you must strive for as a person.

As an example, jumping off to porn has the same brain chemical processes that are involved in having real sexual sex. Video games or watching sports can make you feel like you've mastered physical skills. Watching videos and reading posts make you feel like you've gained valuable knowledge.

This means that it is not just that you aren't working towards those goals in the present, but also there is no need to take them on within the next few months since they're marked as "done" on a to-do lists in your mind.

It's a bit unrealistic to say that you shouldn't indulge in activities that feel good. But, if the preferred pleasure is increasing to the point of totally substituting with the "real things" which you should be striving towards as a person, it's time to get rid of it.

If you're not working toward a romantic relationship due to the fact that porn is your thing it is time to do something drastic to reduce or stop your consumption of porn. If video games are your way of feeling like an incredibly hot girl, then you have get rid of it, take a trip, and perform something truly outrageous. If sports are what keeps you physically well-rounded, you'll need switch off your TV and do something active. The life isn't meant to be lived in front of the screen.

Chapter 12: Wannabe Gigachad

Samuel is a kind of Simp who is aware that he's an Simp however he tries everything to his power to not be an Simp. Samuel gets tattoos in order to look good, is at the gym in order to make your body looking attractive to the women, and purchases a brand-new Mercedes to appear rich, even though it's not. The whole thing started at the gym where a lady wanted to know if he was able to find her at the bench press. They began talking, and then they started exercising with each other. The man has made it. He found himself a beautiful girl who first approached him. The self-improvement efforts ended up paying off. He thought at the very least. His workouts started to lose their effectiveness because his focus was on aiding her rather than his own schedule of training. He started to modify her exercise routine which was mainly concentrated on strengthening the glutes, with no exercises for the upper body like women typically prefer to perform. He soon decided to stay at her side at the gym. He was determined to show everyone that the woman "belonged" to him, so she would not be able to talk to anyone else. He would not even say hello to his buddies in the presence of her. He was afraid that they would be talking to her, and she may take a connection with their company. The girl once told her that she believed an individual in the gym was appealing. A man with a beard who was a lot taller that our Simp. She went on to say that she was more interested in these bulky males. Our Simp however was on the thinner part. Although he wasn't overweight, the guy wasn't super-slim either. He had been working towards getting an eight-pack prior to. However, after hearing about this, his plan has changed. He was determined to gain weight. He wanted to build. He began eating more and stuffed his face and attempting to eat 5000 calories per day. for a man of his size, this was an enormous over-consumption that could result in the majority of people gaining weight. Then our Simp friend and a girl began making plans to hook up. The lights were required to be turned off for the act she requested. She was not a fan of being around him. She didn't like him. Our Simp seemed naive, and assumed that it was because of how she felt about it, or perhaps she was just a bit timid. The girl soon began making demands. If the Simp would like to have a chance on her it was imperative that he give her something. Make her a reservation for a delicious meal or purchase her a gift. Anything she wants the day. The reason she was using sex was as an instrument to influence the man to make him perform something to her. In essence, she was using it to influence her. When it was time to committing the crime her attitude was completely uninterested over it, and wanted to move on. The girl was talking to another man at the gymnasium. They were always sexy with her eyes seeking the next chance. Then she'd start training with a young man. Naturally, it was an exercise session and nothing to get jealous of she said to that to our Simp her friend. Our Simp became extremely jealous and threatened him that he must leave her alone. The guy eventually became exhausted from dealing with the issue and decided to stop working with her. Following the incident, the girl, unhappy, stated that she wanted to take to take a break. Everything became way too excessive for her. The Simp was forced to take the girl's decision. Perhaps he was reacting too strongly He thought. He wanted to put in every efforts to get the girl's affection. After a while, the girl began exercising with a guy known as Chad. Chad was large, tall beautiful, attractive, and powerful. The perfect person we as a Simp was hoping to be however, he was not. Soon after, they were couples. Then she realized that she no longer needed to rest when the perfect man came in. He was her all-time crush and posted his picture on her social networks and acted in a very submissive manner around the guy. She didn't even look at the other men on the treadmill and started dressing in less-revealing clothing and had oversized shirts covering her tummy. In the meantime, Chad was concentrating on his business, he was concentrating on his work out. The Simp was heartbroken but did not give up hope of being back together one day. It is possible that she will get tired of the latest Chad person and see that Chad was the best option. Perhaps he was just looking to grow a bit and maybe put on some amazing tattoos that were a bit more sexy or even get a cooler car. He wanted to win her back someday. It's been a while time is now past and our Simp discovered a cute woman at Uni. He had been interested in her for a considerable amount of time and was delighted at the chance that allowed him to finally open with her in a meaningful dialogue. It was the same scenario repeated. After having been with her for two weeks, she was in need of an escape. Again. The Simp had been shocked. He wasn't sure what he could've done more effectively. The new tats were put on and he grew bigger and he had perfect teeth yet it was not sufficient... However, there was there was one thing he wasn't changing not at all. His inner beliefs as well as his attitude, desire for attention, his jealousy and insecurity. He also had a insecurity... Even with every effort to improve the way he thought, he was still an Simp. There's nothing wrong with having all the look and the money in this world, but if your attitude unchanging and you're still a simp internal. It's just a way to hide your real self. It is essential to have a mentality of prosperity. It is essential to be certain of the value you bring to your life. It is important to think: "It is her loss If she decides to leave me, I'm the one who wins." It is a fact that it is possible to find a woman superior, submissive, better looking than her at any time. Don't make yourself change to a woman, you take it on yourself. If she loves it cool, great, and if she doesn't, equally amazing. People will be drawn to it and consider your appealing. It's not likely for every woman around the globe will consider your attractive. That's fine. There's a lot of people who will. Even if you do not meet a woman like this in a short time you'll still feel like you're satisfied by your goal. Women are just an added value to your lifestyle, a source of joy but not the whole of your life. When you are in this state, it is impossible to tolerate any kind of disdain. If the Simp was a person of prosperity and placed his goals prior to anything else, he may behave differently. He would not have been angry at this woman who was working out in the fitness center. What happens if guys glance at her. This means she's hot. The guy wouldn't be bothered. He's so engaged in himself, or at a gruelling pace, and has no time or desire to fret for a better match. If she finds someone better then, it's her loss. Since in his eyes there is a prize for him. He is aware of his worth. If she believes somebody is better for her than she is, then she's free to go with her. He is aware that there are females who will appreciate the worthiness of him. There's nothing to gain... Just one girl who wasn't attracted to himself in the first place. What is the reason he would want to spend time with this girl even if he didn't want to? The sex and relationship are not passionate. What woman believes that she is rewarding you by sleeping with her. You should want to be intimate with you just as you share it with her, or more. Stop slacking and begin thinking of yourself as a prize!

Supreme gentleman

The festival we attended was together, which is effectively five people you'd call Alpha and one would be a Simp. In this setting, where there were Alphas but he still went through the motions of the Simp. He was trying to be part of with the crowd, but his many years of simping made him the person he is, so that he could not pretend to be an Alpha for long. Therefore, Andrew was a new single However, he was surrounded by females. Two of them also were attending the event and were fighting for interest. He was unaware that he'd be able to meet the two girls who he had to deal with however he didn't really care. He is the man who is coveted by women of other genders and that the fear of competition among these girls will increase his appeal to these girls. Andrew did not stop drinking and did not give two women the time of the day. This is where we bring our Simp in the game. He noticed two women who were in the crowd and suggested that he buy them drinks. It's the way a true man should be like, act as an obedient gentleman or so he believed. He continued to purchase beverages throughout the entire time whenever they wanted to refill. There was no need to speak up. When he realized that they were left with nothing they had, he brought them another round of beverages. In the course of time the Simp walked up to one girl and told her that Andrew was in love with the woman, he just was not showing the signs. Andrew was later aware of this and was furious. how could the Simp fabricate such false statements and raise the hopes of a girl? Andrew screamed at the Simp. The

Simp was hesitant to claim that he loved this girl, or maybe the fact that he didn't think of himself as worthy enough to look into a relationship to be with her. The party ended with Andrew leaving. Andrew found a new girlfriend who he brought back home. The rest of the guys in the group left as well in groups or with women. The Simp was with the two girls. The Simp accompanied them home to ensure they were safe. After arriving at the home, the girls walked in with a tearful goodbye with the Simp and closed the door behind the Simp. The time was past midnight, and the Simp was exhausted and the girls were unable to offer him a room. Therefore, he left the home. He said he'd take them to the airport on next day's celebration. festivities. After a whole day of serving as a butler for them and their guests, they wouldn't let him sleep on the sofa. He grew tired, became very sleepy, and lay down to sleep and fell asleep on the balcony of the apartment. On the next day, he joined his friends to the next celebration and arranged for the transportation. What a gentleman. He gave his life for two strangers who didn't really care about him. He lay on the cold and dirty floor of the banister. He and spent an enormous amount of money drinking and was a security guard as well as butler. But for what? What was he offered for his efforts? Perhaps an "thank for your time"? It's unlikely he received the slightest hint of that. What kind of man and respect for others, do that? That's not what it means to be the definition of a gentleman. Simply being the definition of a Simp. The sacrifice of oneself to get the attention of girls who are not worth it and getting nothing back. Would you like to be the same way? Would you prefer to have the role of Andrew who had two girls competing to get his attention on the following day even though Andrew left the scene with a different girl? You decide. Doing "nice" to be nice to impress others won't get you far on the planet, particularly with women. Make sure you put your own needs and wants first. It's not worth purchasing drinks for girls who aren't yours. They will not respect you. Don't give your attention, your validation, your money for free. What did they do to merit it? Because they're female? Be more like Andrew. Be yourself and have fun. Don't be a slave to show off, just make sure you are confident in your abilities and let the ladies chase at you. Don't be a slouch and just take care of what is best for you!

The puffywhipped

Most men when they are in an intimate relationship, begin to put women on the place of honor and becoming the woman's servant. They get rid of all their plans, passions, friendships and ambitions out the out of the. It's typical Simp conduct. Our next instance shows that our Simp coworker Matthew required him to end contact with his friends after the relationship began with his girlfriend. The friends of his would have adversely influencing him, his girlfriend said. Naturally, he agreed to it. her wishes were his commands. He was the queen, after all. When he began spending his spare time with her He renounced all of his interests and acquaintances. He became her animal. Prior to meeting, our Simp was very interested in exercising boxing, and was committed to improving his skills. He was a social circle where he was well-known and loved. He had a lot of energy and had a radiance of confidence. He was very attractive to females. It was how he drew noticed by his present lover. However, once they were one couple, the committed motivated man she was in love with became the size of a puppy. The tiger was put down. It had turned into a household cat slowly, but gradually. Some women think that they need to have a partner who will live their life to the sake of them, one who offers her all their attention and puts their needs first. The man is expected to slack off the gym so that they can relax in their bed with a cuddle or go on Netflix. It is possible that they will say they are fond of your appearance with some extra fluffy, an extra to hold on. In reality, they're trying to discredit you to women who are not as attractive so that they are able to relax and not have to worry about being a victim of competitors. This is how our Simp was tricked too. He was once fit and strong, but the guy was now skinny and weighty. In the past, there was a need to visit the barber on a regular basis to have a new haircut. He now only goes once every two weeks. He did not want to leave. He used to drive his girlfriend each day to work, and later take her home. He had a life to please his girlfriend. There was no reason for him any more, but he believed that they were both happy and loved. A short time was passed, and the girl began to get increasingly irritable and naive. The girl began to demand more. She began to insult him, saying to make him look like a fake man. She basically lost all love toward him. He was no longer the person who caused her to be drawn to him initially. The fit, motivated and goal-oriented guy wasn't him anymore. The woman began to crave other men. They were tough athletic and fit. And quickly she was able to cheat on him with a guy. It was a stalemate. Our Simp defeated. He lost his girlfriend and himself. He was in poor shape and depressed. He was without money in be able to relocate back home with his parents. Then he reached out to his friends via his Facebook pages (he was not permitted to take part in any social interactions in his relationship) and explained what had was going on. He explained that the blame was on him because she was such an amazing girl, but that he was not mature enough. The cycle then repeated its self. He then got another woman two years later, and has the same mistake now. There are many men today who belong to the Simp group. They're focused on what they do in their lives, doing the right thing until they get to get to know someone that they truly love, they toss all their ambitions out the out of the window. A saying states: "Give a weak man constant sex, healthy food and entertainment at a low cost, and he'll dump all his goals right out the out of the window." Don't be too relaxed with a partner. You were the person you were before getting a girlfriend will have to remain the same as a man when you find yourself an attractive girl. You have to work harder. If you wish to remain attracted to a girl You must keep growing. Naturally, you are doing it by yourself but being aware of this will give you less motivation to be confident. Females themselves may not even realize that they consider these features appealing. You might think that she'd rather you not do exercise for instance to watch Netflix and have pizza with her. In reality, she sees an attractive man who is focused and well-organized. He is able to resist lazyness as well as comfort and will say NO to the Netflix session, because he has to exercise or start a side business. He'll keep improving in pursuit of his goals and will appeal all women but not only to the lady that he's currently in a relationship with. It will cause her to experience fear of competition. She is afraid of losing her man to a prettier woman. Therefore, she is doing the work and treating her husband more well, and making her healthier and attractive so that men will continue to find her appealing. The woman will be at her most professional conduct. She'll behave with respect as she has a guy who clearly is a powerful leader and doesn't let his ego get in the way. Their relationship are harmonious, the woman is in her gentle, female energy, and the man is in his protective powerful, driven masculine spirit. Therefore, stop slacking off and start placing your goals and self before all else, even if you do get yourself a woman!

Chapter 13: Ghosted

A few days ago, Tristan thought of downloading Tinder. He got tired of heading to the bar every week and spending a lot of cash on drinks for random ladies, and even giving up his sleep and then going back home empty handed. He realized that most women in the club visit to enjoy complimentary drinks and attention to boost their confidence and go home with a bad-boy sort of man who does not show them much interest. Perhaps through using an online dating site, his odds were better to go for a one-on-one date with the woman. He began to set up his profile. He picked a photo of him at the gym and appearing pretty and confident on his profile picture. There were a few other photos of him on the move and playing with his fellow boys. He began swiping at the girls. There were a lot of women he thought were attractive however he wasn't able to connect with any. He noticed the fact that most of these girls put their Instagram details in their descriptions of their profiles, suggesting that they could be found through the app. Therefore, he began DMing those girls there as well. But the girls didn't respond to him. He figured they might have been unable to contact them because they hadn't seen them. He began following them his friends, likes and comments on the entire content of theirs. One girl even responded to a post of his by using the heart emoticon. It was beginning to get somewhere and thought he was on the right track. When he attempted to initiate a conversation the conversation was interrupted once more. He continued to swipe on Tinder each day. He came across one of those profiles that looked mysterious and had just one picture. The profile was called Cherry. The photo shows that you can barely make out the face. the image was cropped and only the lips of her were clearly visible. Her body was slender with a beautiful bra and hourglass shape, large hips as well as a small waist. Her profile stated: "I don't like presenting myself on the internet. If I'm a fan then you will view more pictures of me." Tristan first thought it was an untrue profile from a strange dude who is that was baiting guys. However, he was still fascinated and swiped the right way. A few minutes after... There was the perfect game. This girl had swiped at him as well. He immediately began messaging her and they soon exchanged Snapchats. He asked her for her contact number at first however she replied that she wasn't going to give him her phone number immediately He had to get it. She sent him some photos of her as well. Tristan loved what he read. They planned a Saturday night date. He'd to her home. The place she lived wasn't too distant from him. When the wedding day, when he appeared in front of her house the girl walked out and she was embraced by him. Her appearance was stunning in real life and was also beautiful in person. Tristan felt relieved. He was concerned that he might be being cat-fished. The two began walking through the neighborhood, walking in an unlit park. They sat in a trance, and had a excellent conversations. She was working out and working out, too. They were also talking about this. about hobbies, work and other things, and how long they'd been using Tinder. The woman said that she installed the application that day when they began messaging. She was unaware of the app. She was just told by her friends that she download it. They then began talking about previous relationships. His last romance ended one year earlier. The man said that they'd just separated. The woman said that her previous affair was just a few months ago. The two broke up just around a month ago according to her explanation. Tristan did not think about the break-up once more. The two continued to walk as they got closer and closer to one another. They stared each other into the eyes. Then he went to the kiss. The two began to make out. He was in awe and felt very attracted by her. Her smartwatch suddenly began constant ringing. He jokingly asked if she was a jealous ex boyfriend calling. However, to his shock, she told him the call was indeed from her ex-boyfriend. Her ex-partner was required to collect items that were still in her home. Therefore, she had to head to her home right now. She walked out and told Tristan that she'd make her return in the future time and also if he did not be angry over the incident. Tristan said that it was not a huge issue and they went on to say goodbye and she headed to her home. When they arrived at home, Tristan was thinking about the possibility that she could not have been that keen on the guy. Perhaps it was an excuse to escape from him. It is likely that she had some of her acquaintances reaching out to her in order to help get out of the circumstances, he thought. He was surprised to receive a call from her right after. The two had exchanged phone numbers over the time. She wanted to know if she was safe and home. He was happy. He and his girlfriend started to text and scheduled a date within the next week. A couple of days passed, and He noticed he wasn't seeing her profile photo no longer. Did he get blocked? Did she alter her decision? The day before the date, he was able to see her profile on the internet. He inquired if there was a date available at the time. He was told "Of Of course! We'll see us later." He was invited to stay with her at home. She provided him with a bizarre guide to the address he needed to go to, and requested him to not turn on the lights or refrain from making noise. As he walked into her home, she was lit up with red LEDs along with a television playing music. The woman offered him a drink and then asked "Shall us continue from the way we left off?" They started making out, and then he started stripping her. She was dressed in sexy and seductive intimate lingerie. She was definitely into him. The girl started to feel her abs and was praising his fitness level. was. Then another thing happened and soon they were engaging in sexual sex. Tristan was so cute and decided to not use a condom. The girl was not bothered by it neither. About 20 minutes later and the girl began to check her watches. She declared "Let's not go on longer Okay?" Tristan continued to take her to the ground in various positions until he finished his breasts. She told her to get him out of the way as her ex-boyfriend would come back. He wanted to go with the dog on an outing. Therefore, he dressed fast and left to take a shower. He then left her home. The two continued talking between time to time but she became insecure, so at some point, the connection slowed down and she began to ghost the guy. He was really fond of her, and thought they had a great chemistry. What is the reason she would snub him? His performance surely wasn't lacking neither. After some research, he discovered her Facebook page in which he found some photos of her as well as a man. He recognized the man as her former boyfriend. However, what he observed was that there was no evidence of their relationship ever ending. They had photos of them together in the time that they were in a relationship.

Explanation:

The girl was cheating with her boyfriend. They had been together for a significant period of time over 7 years. He began accusing her of being cheating, but she did not have any evidence. She began manipulating herself to believe that he was doing something illegal. She began telling her peers about the incident. They told her that If he was able to have enjoyable with girls she ought to as well. She was also enticed to sign up for Tinder to see whether there were any attractive males. Naturally, she wouldn't want to use an image that could possibly be recognized by acquaintances that were friends with her partner. Therefore, she created a "mystery" account. The relationship was becoming dull in their relationship, however she wasn't ready to split up just yet since they had been living quite well. Then she became our close friend Tristan. The weekend evening, her boyfriend would arrive to work late. This was also the time to meet with other guys and also with Tristan. When she was out with her boyfriend, she would try to block Tristan to make sure he was unable to reach her, so that she would be unable to get snatched in the eyes of her lover. When she fell in love with Tristan and had sexual relations in his presence, she was becoming a bit guilty. The desire to test a different dick had been at its peak. She began to e-mail the guy and pretending that nothing took place. The boyfriend had no idea.

Beware of the girls you meet using dating websites, particularly ones with no profile. There is a good chance that they are involved in a relationship or going through a break is significant. They are looking to do new things without being in trouble or simply enjoy some diversity and joy within their lives. They also don't give out their phone number. So it is not possible to call or message their number if they're in a relationship with their boyfriend. A lot of girls have relationship breakups due to this. It is common for them to tell their partners that their lives have become excessive lately and that they're in need of some time to themselves. The time away is a good time to spend. Particularly, it is spent with your fellow men. They move from one guy to the next man until they have the thrill they crave. If she can't find a partner she believes could make an ideal long-term partner then she'll go back with her companion and appear like it was never happening. This cycle repeats at times when they are bored. This allows them to cheat and not feel guilty. In the event that she falls in love with a different guy in the time that she is in love with, she'll keep dating until she's certain that the person she is dating is also interested in being involved with her. Then she'll begin discontinuing contact with her old partner entirely. If you're in a scenario with a woman who has recently broken up (more than likely they're in a break) it is a good chance of them coming to a reunion. You can either stay away of such women or pretend to be the girl and enjoy yourself with no expectations. Be aware of the reasons why she's becoming sluggish or beginning to appear ghostly, once the situation occurs.

Chapter 14: Unforgettable

A time I was having a drink with my coworkers in the club. There was one Simp hidden within the crowd who was caught fairly swiftly. The dance floor was full of people enjoying ourselves when a obese girl started throwing her sex at us all by one. She was drinking heavily and wanted attention. The group was not a swarm of people who was willing to give her the time throughout the day. she was ostracized. The Simp was starting to get up on her, seemingly thrilled by the fact that he had an average girl. The two went in the smoking section and sat around with each with each other. There's nothing wrong with having pleasure with these girls at the club, however anyone who would like to be taken more seriously, especially with one who was able to run by half of the men must have his head examined. After the night, the Simp brought the girl back home to sleep in his crib. Later that day, the Simp was proud to tell his Whatsapp group of how wonderful his time with the girl was and how much it was a pleasure to have sex with her. Following that, he tried to woo her several times throughout the week, however she didn't respond to anything. The Simp was unable to understand and the two of them came to meet in the same place over the weekend. He was already hoping to meet her once more. He walked up to her, asking if she'd like to go dancing with him but she replied that the person whom she was in with has a slight illness and she needed to care for her. Evidently, it was an excuse. It's likely that the evening wasn't so great as the Simp believed it was or at least for her. After a while, the Simp was seen again together with her group of friends in the opposite area of the club. They were having a blast, there were two men were also there. The Simp attempted to win again and began to approach the crowd and began dancing with her. The Simp didn't seem to get the clue. The girl was irritated. She got up, excused herself from her group of friends, and then went off to the bathroom. The entire group of friends then told that Simp to leave the girl to her own devices, as There were plenty of other females in the room. Was he in love over her? He said that their evening in love was truly memorable... it's likely that she was drinking an excessive amount of alcohol and was not feeling well. He was still living in his fantasies. After an hour, the Simp noticed the girl at another location dancing and kicking at two males. He was angry and emotional. What could she do? He walked up to her in tears, and begged for her to talk with him fast. A couple of guys shoved the man away and asked that he should leave. He remained persistent, and began pulling her by the arm in order to talk to her outside without interruption. The girl was fed up and began to smack him like one of her t-shirts across the face. "How did you do that?", he cried, "I thought we had something very special... I'm hurting my heart". The man with her shoved him back. The security arrived to the scene, grabbed the Simp and took him out of the bar. The man was devastated and started crying. He attempted to call her on her cell phone and she refused the phone call. He then wrote her a note: "Delete all the pictures as well as memories that we shared." The Simp was then shut down. The Simp was shattered through a fat local. The moral is to not try to marry the hoe. Like she was before you, she'll continue to be there for you. It's fun to slut, but they're not the only thing. Stay on the move. It's normal to expect that they'll not stay faithful to you. Most likely, you won't see your wife of the future at the bar. Keep your expectations low. A year afterwards it was discovered that the Simp discovered the girl via the Dating App and apologized for his conduct, hoping that he might get another opportunity. The girl responded: "No worries" and was a ghost afterward. Some guys never learn. Don't be one of them. Be aware of your value and commit you to the highest standard. Do not settle for just any woman. Be careful!

Uber driver Uber driver

An employee was constantly driving our car home after work since our house was on the way. There was no cash or any other thing from us. It was just a matter of good friends It was just natural. As a reward, we might do his other favours. The man was praised for his work. A 19 year young woman at work who looked pretty decent but wasn't much of a standout. Everyone was swooning for her as did our coworker. Our friend was couple in his early 30s. She always took the bus when she returned after work. The other day, our Simp friend came to us, and told us that the bus was not able to take us to home that night. We didn't owe him anything and maybe he was just trying to collect his wife or some other thing. We didn't get mad, and did not doubt it any further. We later learned that he took that girl who was 19 to her home. A complete opposite direction to where the majority of his time. In two weeks, he'd return home to the woman without any compensation. He would spend his time and cash for the girl... to what purpose? To get her attention, feel her company or receive an extra "thank to you"? The only Simp can do this for girls simply because she's beautiful. Making her his time. If that wasn't enough for his wife, she discovered that he had been taking her back to her home all the time and that's his reason for being returning home earlier than normal. He would be lying to his wife to tell her that it was because he worked a bit of extra work. His wife later separated from him. The fact that he was sexy for another woman was a complete turn off for her. This wasn't just due to the fact that he was cheating. After discovering that her husband was an unreliable Simp who didn't care about his personal time... her was unable to respect him at all. He was essentially just an Uber driver for a 19-year-old girl, and didn't get any money in exchange. If he had even one of her lovers, it's less than a pity. He didn't leave her due to cheating rather because he smacked himself as the Simp. Women will be able to forgive an Alpha male to cheat, but she will have no respect for a guy who simps for another. It is not a good thing to be being a sexy partner. This is a losing situation.

Love knows no distance

The idea of long-distance romance isn't making sense for a premium man. If you're not able to have instant access to her sexual pleasures the girl, she's not a good candidate for a romantic relationship. Keep in mind this statement. In the next tale, the Simp friend was two years of relationship with his high school love interest. He was absolutely over her, and they shared a very good relationship. He thought that at the very the very least. At the time that I got to know him, he shared with me that his daughter had left for university and she'd be studying in a different nation. I looked him in the eye with a critical look. The man continued... and with the slightest smile. He'd purchase a ticket every 3 months, to go out to see her, he told her. Maybe two years down the line it could be that she would return to study here for a while as he believed. I was just listening and thinking to myself that it's only one time until she found a local male. Every young woman anywhere in the world can go that long without having a sex. There aren't any celibate angels. They're as hot like men, sometimes more. It is ludicrous to think that the mere sight of one another every three months is enough. A couple of months had gone by of them texting and conversing almost everyday before the girl began to become ever more irritable. Every time she had an excuse to explain why she wasn't able to chat with him as often more. She needed to go out with her group of learners or take different classes. A few days later, the girl called our Simp friend to inform him that she felt abandoned by the man. The girl wanted to put things behind her. She believed they haven't been able to get along, but he remained charming person, and were able to remain friends if would like. The Simp friend was heartbroken and was willing to keep the friendship going, believing about how he would revive her feelings when she returned to her home. It was only a week and she had already posted stories and sharing them with a fellow local smiling and having fun. Evidently, the Simp was blocked from seeing the stories, however there were people who were friends with them that saw their posts and they told the Simp. In less than two weeks later the incident, she had posted a photo of her and the guy she met on her Facebook page. The Simp was heartbroken. She was unable to come into contact with a different man after just a brief period of time. In the meantime, the Simp stood by his side and made not spoken to any other woman in the dream of his proposal after she had returned. The Simp's world was ruined. It is a rule of thumb you should be aware of. Women fall out mentally long prior to breaking into physical relationships. When they break apart, they must locate a new replacement, a different man, and they need to make sure that he will be a better choice that her lover. When she went to a different country for university and showed how her work was much more important over her relationship with him. Someone who was attracted to a guy will abandon her own personal ambitions to just be together with him. They would not let go of their lover for this long time because she was afraid of losing her. Therefore, she had made her decision that she wasn't all that interested in her lover. It's only an issue of time until she met another one who was more suitable and close by. It is likely that she had already had a conversation with him during the very beginning of her uni days and was with him for time time prior to breaking up with our young Simp. The long-distance relationship offers nothing to gain for a person who is highly valued and has an abundance-minded mindset. What can a woman offer him if she lives all over the globe? So why should he take two years off for a lady who willingly abandons him to pursue a career or school or whatever. It's not worth such. When she took the choice to walk away the man should have stated: "I don't do long distant relationships. Please take good time, let's cut off when you're for another visit." Then he would make the relationship casual for a while or cut contact entirely. Any other alternative makes him look like a Simp. There are so many gorgeous women around the globe. There is no need to be or remain in a affair with a woman that you see only at least once a month. Don't do this and waste your time by entering into or remaining in a long-distance relationship. Do not be fooled!

Chapter 15: Stop Simping Rules

Don't exchange money for love!

The most important thing be aware of is that genuine love cannot be purchased. Do not fall for the trap of using your assets and money to attract a woman who is not yours. If you make a statement that is based on this then they'll be attracted to them for their money and not as an individual. They'll try to trick you in order to extract more of your money. They'll use sex to get presents in exchange the opportunity to take them to the mall or pay for their expenses. If you are unable to pay the bills it is a sure way to lose ladies, in this case because they were not attracted to the person you were, rather more in the things you can provide to their needs. Similar to automobiles and clothes. A lot of young men are prone to spending their entire money on costly clothes or automobiles in the hope of attracting many women in this way. Most of the time people fail since they're doing too much. Making an effort to be a hit will show vulnerability and women are able to smell the energy of this person from miles away. Making yourself appear more valuable will only get the job done but only to a certain extent. You must work on your confidence in yourself, your charisma, on your interpersonal skills, and cash is the top of the cake. It's much more attractive If you let women discover about the car by themselves. Be discreet. Instead of splurging every penny on designer clothes, you should get your body perfect first. Get in shape, become strong, lean and muscular and buy some good fit clothes that appear better than an unfit guy who spends his entire cash on fancy designer brands. It's much more enjoyable for you to sleep with women who really love the person you are and consider you beautiful. This is why purchasing women will not make you completely happy. It's not exactly the same... passionate and sexy. The affection and love will be a bit fake. It is common to see an old overweight man with plenty of money seduce young gorgeous women. Consider Are they actually finding him appealing? Does he have any enthusiasm in intimacy? Is it more of the transaction of giving the women his possessions and exchange it for sexual pleasure that is not passionate? He uses them for funds, and maybe share some photos on their Instagram about how they're wearing an Bugatti or on a boat but that's all. They still want different types of men who have a good physique and are attractive. It is not a good idea to find yourself trapped in such a scenario. So, you must only purchase things that you need to yourself. Only if you are able to really afford the items. Better to accumulate your savings at an early stage and then build your own business, or even invest in training courses.

You can be a leader!

A Simp will ask what woman would like to accomplish or the place she would like to go for a meal. It is true that women tend to be less decisive as males. It's tiring for them to choose what they want. They don't know the food they'd like to eat or what they would like to accomplish. What they don't want to have is a guy who's equally undecisive. It's a recipe to disaster. When you ask her "What you'd like to do?" , she replying "I do not know what could we accomplish?" and you saying "Hmmm whatever you like." You'll get nowhere. Then you'll lose all attraction, and be way too to handle for her.

She would like to be guided. Go on an adventure with her and make it thrilling. Make her the driver and you be the driver.

She can guess which direction you'll be taking her. She should be thrilled about the idea. Do not let her utilize any of her brainpower the ability to think of ideas for what you might accomplish. You're looking to get your girlfriend out, didn't you? Now, it's your responsibility to create a memorable experience. You must be an effective the leader. Be decisive. You are the Captain of the vessel. You will be able to distinguish yourself from the rest of the undecisive Simps. This is the same for dating a girl to go out on a date. You should plan everything ahead on the things you'll accomplish. What activity, or what you're taking her to dinner. Set up a plan so that you don't appear confused and unsure. Make sure she is present at a particular time and also if she needs to wear a nice dress or something more casual. There's nothing else she has to think about. She'll trust her life to the people you trust.

Stop begging for sex!

"Honey is it okay this evening?" Your wife/girlfriend: "If you do this... and ..., may be the chance to have luck later tonight." What a tinny way is that? Being lucky? What is it that makes you lucky? The ability be able to sleep with your partner or spouse. It's a matter of luck to be able to do it? It's a fact for the majority of males today. They were brainwashed by television shows that feature Simp male characters who need to plead for a date in their personal relationships with wives. This is an entire Simp dynamic. The woman you choose to marry should want for your appearance and desire to satisfy you. Females love sex just as like men, if perhaps much... when they're with the right person. The man who is worth it doesn't have to fulfil all desires just so that they can be "lucky". Women throw their weight around him. The guy doesn't have to be doing or saying any thing. Don't ever ask for sexual sex. If you are being in the position that it is necessary to actually request it. Take the time to think about it. It's not right when it got to the present. It is likely that you have set her up on the pedestal and made her feel like the one to be admired. She is now riding high and believes she is that she is entitled. The sex she has had is now higher important than yours. Are you on goals, have you been working out regularly and taking good care about your look? No matter if you're single or part of the course of a relationship, you need to constantly strive to present yourself in the best way. The way you groom yourself, the food you eat as well as your daily visit to your barber, clothing, and your skin care... every aspect should be perfect. So that you stay appealing to your lover, however but you'll be appealing to females around the world as well. If you're that beautiful as you leave your home do you not think that your girlfriend will become worried that you will meet other attractive women who are going to throw their weight at your face? If you're not satisfied and deprived of sexual pleasure what is the likelihood to you'll take action in a way that reflects your feelings? You must now take your sexy balls off prior to leaving the home. They'll treat you well to make sure you'll remember the things you've accomplished at home the next time you see another lovely woman. It's not going to be a case of excuses such as "I had a migraine", "I'm tired" or any other excuse. You will be enticed by her continuously. Do not be shocked if find yourself the one who will get tired after.

Do not have relationship with a long distance!

If you believe that long-distance relationships can work, and you're engaged in one, or would like to join one, you likely have the Simp mentality. The first step is to think about the advantages that you gain from having a long-distance relationship over one that you see one the same day, if you desired. One benefit that I could think of is that it could be possible to have greater time alone. This is out the window for most men because they are spending more time engaging in conversation, playing games as well as making phone calls. But what are the other advantages for a firm and exclusive relationship over long distance? If you get to see one another at least each two weeks or perhaps once each half-year. You don't have any. It is necessary to pay additional money on gas, if you decide to drive there and also pay more for the train ride or even for flights tickets. This is just one of many problems. Imagine that you're financially prosperous and a little amount of money is not really a big deal for your life. Why is there a lack of intimate physical contact? Are you convinced that chats and messaging can substitute for real intimate relationships? Do you think that feeling the warmth of one the other, and smelling and tasting one another? It's not so, I think. How about the sexual aspect? There are weeks or even months before you get lucky? What do you do between? You're slouching to porn? or dirty chatter while you are texting? Are you able to avoid becoming sexually exhausted? Sure, you won't be cheating with her since you're engaged in a committed and faithful relationship. However, do you believe that she'll remain faithful this time also? Are you truly certain? While she's at a night out with friends with a few drinks when a tall, beautiful strong and rich man is spotted approaching her... Are you truly believe she'll be able to remember she had one of the best boyfriends in the world?

There are needs for her as well. The girl is horny too. There is no way to know. You will be contacted by her every day, as if nothing ever happened. It could become something that she does regularly and continues to sleeping with other guys. The whole time even though you're loyal to her. Then, when she discovers herself with someone she likes, you'll become a victim. They will tell you that you and she grew apart and she isn't feeling exactly the same way about her relationship you have with her. It will leave you shocked. And not just that, all of the time that you wasted in your teen years and time chattering and chatting generally having a relationship online that was sexually empty as well as always wondering what she's doing. There are probably gorgeous girls from the area who would be more suitable for you who you can see each all day long if you chose. What's the motivation behind tying yourself to someone who is so in a different place? What is it that makes her special? It is likely that you think she's the most effective you could be. You don't have the mindset of abundance. You're living in a state of scarcity.

Avoid wasting your time or money in long-distance relationships. If you have girls who live a long distance from you, it is possible to have an informal relationship, not more important. It's fine to do it. It is possible to have a blast when you are with each other. Take your thoughts out of it, and focus your mind. Apart from that, you're looking for women to date in your neighborhood.

Value your time!

Simp Simp does not value his personal time. He's on his time. When she had time and he had time. He'll make time to spend time with her. He's always there to help her. When she requires him. What ever she wants him to do. No matter what, he's had work to finish. If she's in need of transportation and needs to get somewhere, the Simp is the one to collect her, and take her to the drop-off point. Unaware of it, he'll take her off at the person she truly wants. Perhaps he's already aware but isn't concerned. In any case, he'll be able to smell a scent of her. Perhaps one day, she'll applaud him and his work are rewarded. So the man hopes. If you're not valuing your personal time and time, then others don't appreciate your time. Do not expect others to. It is essential to be able to articulate an aim, a reason beyond helping women. Someone who is clear on the things he must do and is not disengaged. He can't abandon his task for the sake of playing a chauffeur to impress a girl. He is not going to permit himself to become involved. This would be a betrayal towards himself and his purpose. He will stick to his plan. If the lady follows his schedule or the relationship doesn't be a success. He allows himself time to enjoy being with a lovely and obedient woman after the tasks that had to be completed during the whole week. He will appreciate her in return and appreciate her time more. He knows that he's got work to complete. He's looking to improve within his the world. He is pursuing a goal with a reason and allows her to be part of his mission. He is a Simp's time does not have value; there is no purpose, or any purpose. He who makes time for women does not have any value. His time doesn't matter. He doesn't appreciate her or his time. He is overlooked. Therefore, you should value your time to ensure that your time and, ultimately, your time are valued.

You need principles!

A Simp is a man who has no limits when it comes to relationships. The girl he is with wants to party with his ladies? Fun, enjoy yourself. An excursion on your own to Dubai? - Also, cool. Male friends? Sure but why wouldn't they be only acquaintances. The girl isn't awed by his instincts. The girl he loves would never be a cheater. When she goes to the club, she dances and enjoy herself with other ladies, but she does not care about the guys around her. She dresses in a tight skirt and shows off her cleavage as she loves wearing that style. It's stylish. She isn't a fan of the male focus it attracts sure. She's got a ton of male buddies due to the fact that she is able to get to get along better with guys. It's not a problem They're simply acquaintances. Why wouldn't she contact someone of her acquaintances and ask for a suggestion to Netflix or chill? Maybe they view her as much more than an acquaintance. Perhaps they like her and just want an opportunity to sleep with her? Perhaps they are already however you won't find out. To be a gentleman of worth, it is essential to adhere to a set of principles and establish them when you begin the relationship. If a girl is looking to enter into a serious partnership with you, then she must adhere to the following guidelines. If she doesn't, be casual and fun in your relationship. This doesn't make you better as an individual of worth. You have plenty and you cherish your freedom more than anything other thing. If she is looking to become more committed to you, it's your decision because your dedication will be the reward. This isn't at no cost. There are no girls' nights out and nightclubbing is the primary principle. All of us know the reason girls attend these evenings for girls. They are looking to find out what's new in the market. If they locate a cheaper deal and a superior service. They want the attention they receive. Her single friends can encourage her to participate in the hoe-related events. Women are easily influenced their circle of friends. If her entire group of friends is one-dimensional, slutty girls at parties that should signal a warning to you. Most likely, she is one also. Birds of a Feather flock together. Or she cuts them out to you, or doesn't make a deal with the. Vacations and trips on your own or with friends are prohibited. Many women have a fling with their partners when they are on holiday. The phrase that everyone has heard is "What is happening in Vegas remains the same in Vegas." Nobody is going to find out she has cheated with you in a other country. It's not going to be revealed.

Printed in the USA
CPSIA information can be obtained
at www.ICGtesting.com
CBHW051605171024
15995CB00014B/1180